push forward to the right, against the momentum of everyone
else? Surely they cannot expe
Rather, they seem to be *using*
mass of men into two. They
that follows the direction of t
the back. This break in the pi   ng-hand side
into two triangles. And when I look closer, I notice that the
whole composition is made up of four triangles, though
alongside these principal divisions there are all sorts of other
direction indicators pointing various ways. **”**

Writer Paul Claudel on *The Night Watch*
from *Dutch Painting*, 1935

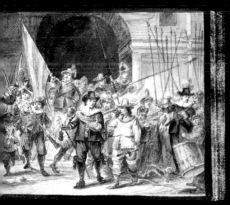

W atercolor copy
of *The Company
of Captain Frans
Banning Cocq*, known
as *The Night Watch*,
showing the painting in
its original state.

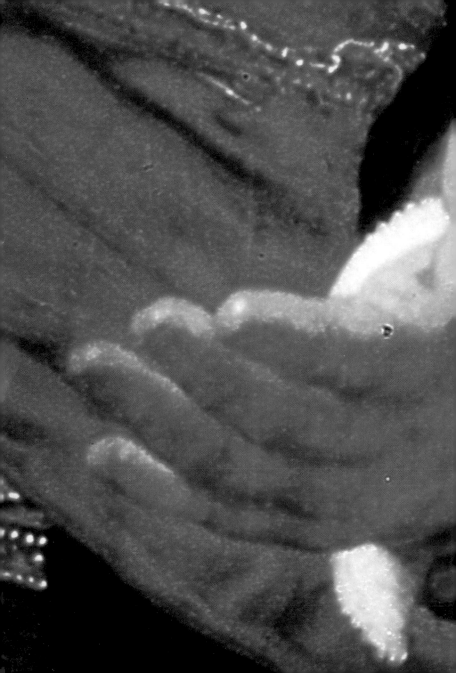

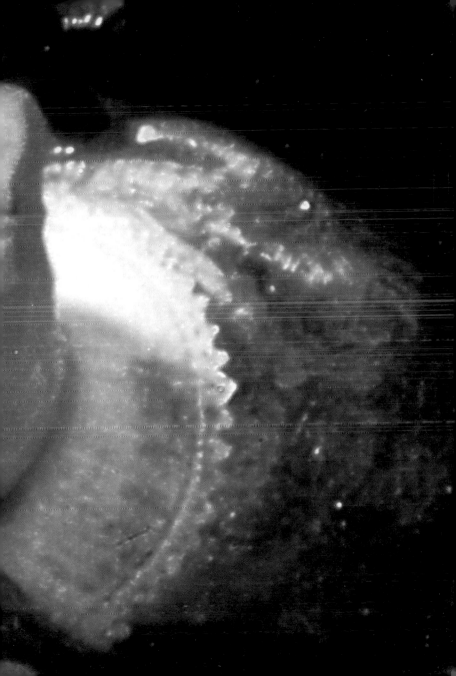

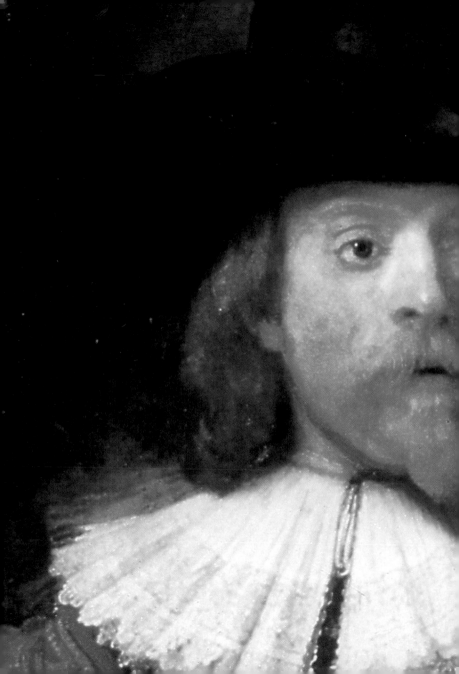

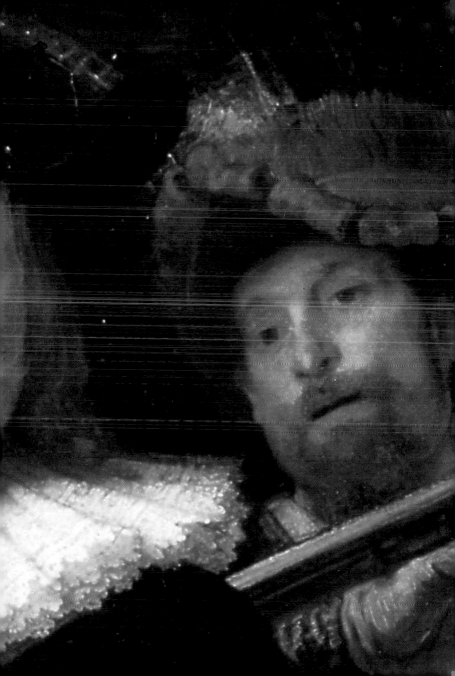

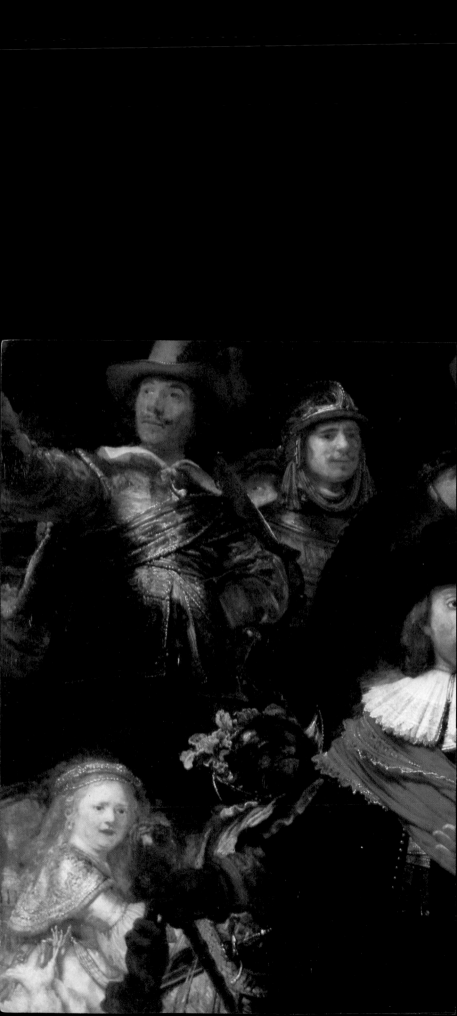

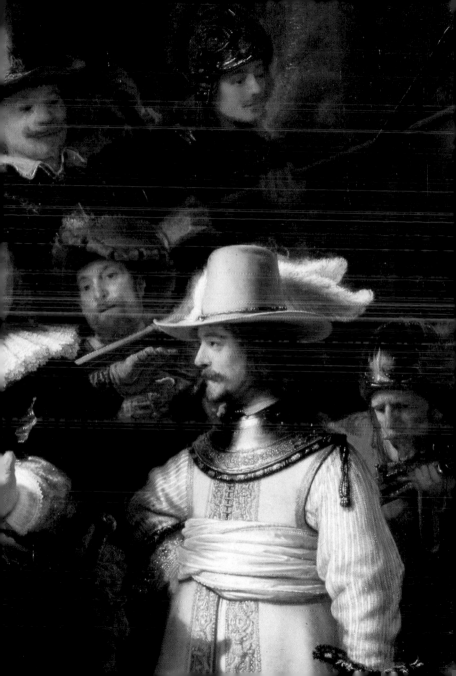

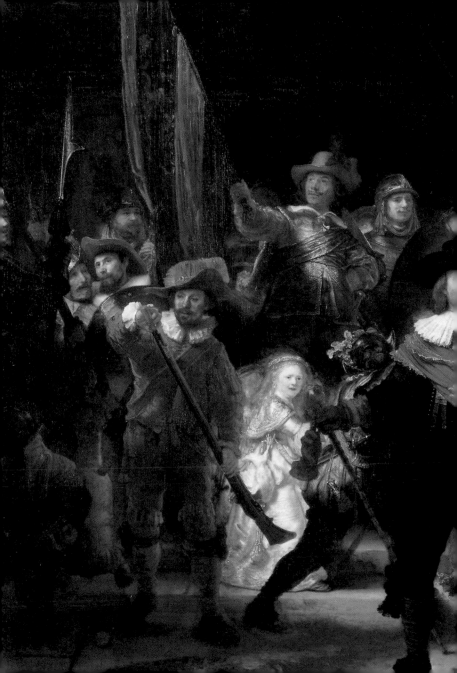

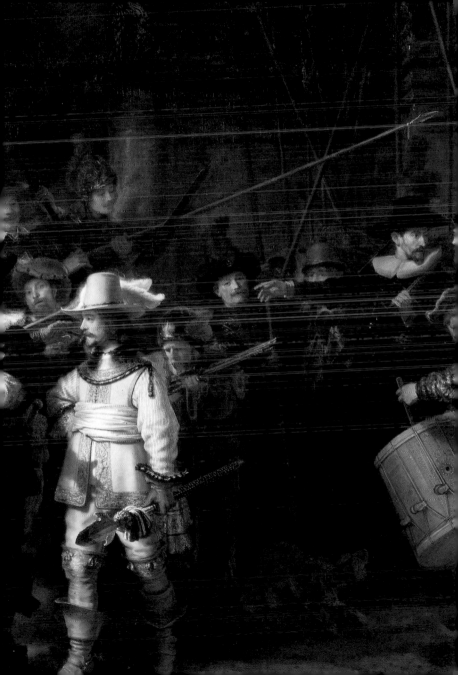

CONTENTS

REMBRANDT
MASTER OF THE PORTRAIT

Pascal Bonafoux

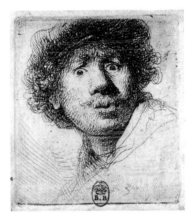

DISCOVERIES

HARRY N. ABRAMS, INC., PUBLISHERS

NEW YORK

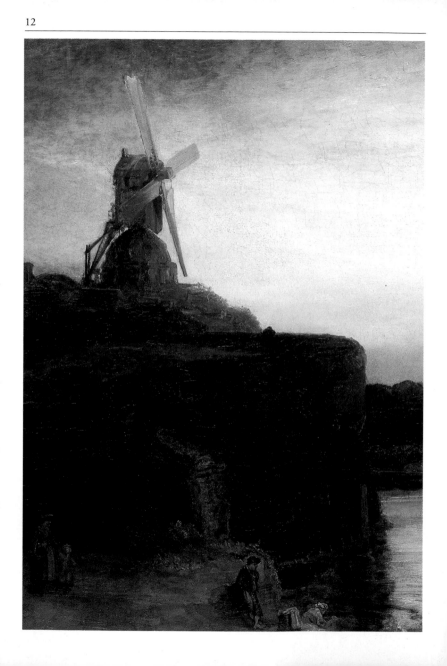

Rembrandt van Rijn, son of Harmen Gerritszoon van Rijn and Cornelia Willemsdochter van Suyttbroeck, was born in Leiden (Holland) on 15 July 1606. Johannes Orlers recorded the fact in a guide to the wonders of Leiden published in 1641. It is the only documentary evidence of the artist's date of birth: We have to accept an element of uncertainty in the tale of his rise to fame and glory.

CHAPTER I

APPRENTICESHIP AND AMBITION

The authenticity of *The Mill* (opposite), long attributed to Rembrandt, is now disputed. There is no doubt, however, about Rembrandt's etching of his father (left), dated 1630.

Harmen Gerritszoon (abbreviated to Gerritsz) van Rijn had married Cornelia Willemsdochter (Willemsdr) van Suyttbroeck on 8 October 1589. Her nickname, Neeltje (or Neeltjen) reveals her to be a baker's daughter.

Harmen Gerritsz was a miller. He took the name van Rijn from the windmill he owned in the northern part of the town on the Weddesteeg, a small street on the embankment of the Oude Rijn, or Old Rhine.

Another branch of the Rhine, the Nieuwe Rijn, forks upriver of the town and flows south of it. Between the two arms of the river lies the network of canals on which Leiden was built. The town numbered some forty thousand inhabitants at the beginning of the 16th century. It had made a successful recovery after the depredations of the Spanish siege of 1574 and, in addition to its industries, boasted a university renowned throughout Europe.

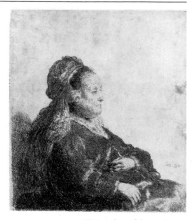

Rembrandt's mother was a frequent and revered model in the artist's Leiden days. This 1631 etching shows her dignified and pensive.

The Van Rijn Family Had Connections with Leiden for Nearly a Century

In 1513 a van Rijn or Vande Rijn was a miller in the town. It is possible that Rembrandt owed his first name to his maternal great-grandmother, Reijmptje Cornelisdr van Blanchem. The name Reijmptje is not unlike Rembrandt, and spelling was not then standardized. A name suggesting a connection with the van Blanchems, an old and prominent family, may well have seemed opportune. Harmen Gerritsz

Leiden, founded in the 9th century, was historically called Lugdunum Batavorum. This plan (opposite) is of the town in 1574, at the end of the Spanish siege. It is shown again (below) as it was in 1601.

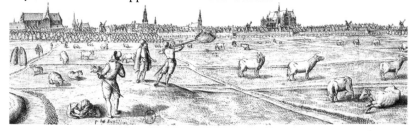

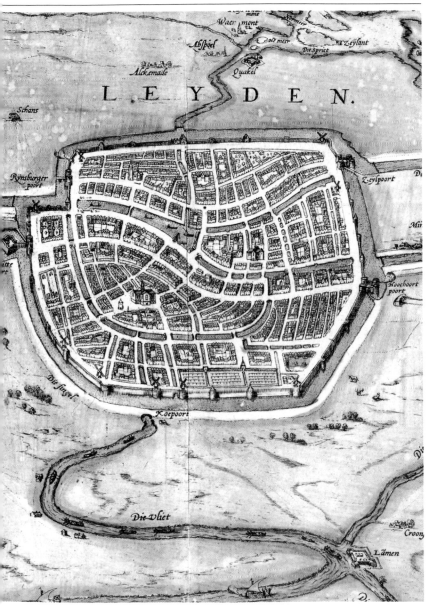

Waer mont

Ahſpoel

ſalt meer Dit Spriet T Zeylant

Alckemade Quakel

L E Y D E N.

Schans

Rynsburger poort

Zeylpoort

De

Mir

Hoochoort poort

Die ſingel

Koepoort

Die Vliet

Croon

Lāmen

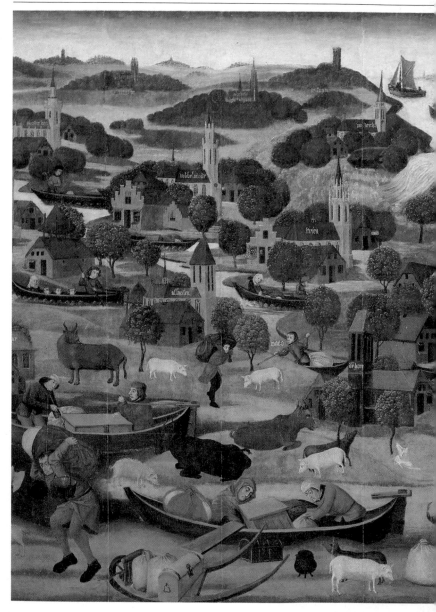

converted to Calvinism, as had Reijmptje, but Rembrandt's mother remained a Catholic.

The van Rijn family was large, as families had to be to survive. Epidemics, disease, and war all took their toll. Rembrandt was the eighth of nine children. The eldest was named Gerrit after his paternal grandfather. Like his father he would be a miller. The second son, Adriaen, became a shoemaker. Three daughters came next, two of whom died young. Rembrandt knew only one of his older sisters, Machteld. Closest to him were his older brothers Cornelis and Willem, both of whom had been born before the turn of the century. After Rembrandt, his mother gave birth to yet another daughter, Lijsbeth.

The family was comfortably off. It is not known whether, when the dikes broke, their mill was requisitioned to pump away the waters flooding the countryside. Harmen would not in any case have hesitated to give what help he could. War, fires in the towns, and the ravages of the North Sea had taught the Dutch solidarity.

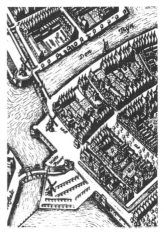

This detail of an early-17th-century map of Leiden shows the Wittepoort district, in which the van Rijn family lived. Their house stood close to the mill, on a little street parallel to the embankment of the Old Rhine.

Fire and Water: Constant and Terrible Enemies

Holland had to defend itself against the sea as it had to defend itself against Spain. In 1606 no truce or treaty had yet been signed. And while the Spanish were one day to retreat, finally granting the United Provinces (the present-day Netherlands) its independence, the sea remained a permanent threat. For hundreds of years the inhabitants of the lowlands, which in the winter months and at very high tides were actually below sea level, had valiantly tried to protect their farms from the sea by building mounds of earth, or dikes; but each year from November to February water seeped in, flooding the country as far as the eye could see. The dikes needed constant reinforcement. Indeed, more men in the country worked keeping the walls of earth in repair than were engaged in tilling the soil. At long intervals numbered posts marked out sections of the dikes, which the villages along the coast were responsible for keeping

A breach in the dike is portrayed in the detail (opposite) of *The St. Elizabeth's Day Flood with Dordrecht in the Background*, an oil painting by a late-15th-century artist known only as the Master of the St. Elizabeth Panels. As the water gushes in through the break at the upper right, men pile their families, livestock, and provisions into boats to escape the flood.

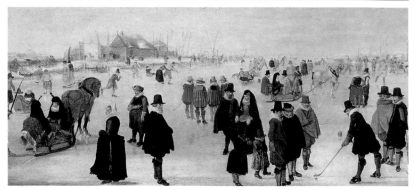

under surveillance. Ceaselessly battered and eroded by the sea, the dikes were the only protection of a country described by a French traveler as "scarcely fit for habitation."

The brick house inhabited by Harmen Gerritsz van Rijn on the Weddesteeg, almost facing his mill, was exactly like the other buildings lining the embankment. Each year, along with his neighbors, Harmen Gerritsz van Rijn would display on his doorstep the buckets and ladders that the town authorities required every citizen to keep in readiness in case of fire. In Leiden, as in all towns in Holland, tar and pitch were used to light the streets and canals. The inevitable fire risk was aggravated by the fact that many houses were built of wood. The townspeople needed to be extremely vigilant.

Pastimes and Prayers

No sooner did winter freeze the canals than the van Rijns took to their skates, as did everyone else—magistrates, preachers, shopkeepers.... Everybody dressed in the same coarse, dark cloth. They played games on the ice with clubs and balls.

The van Rijn family were not puritans who disapproved of the celebration of feast days. They went out with the throng to enjoy themselves, jostling with the best of them. Fiddlers scraped tunes in front of stalls. Tambourines and flageolets (small flutes) were played. There were roars of laughter at the

Picture collectors in the United Provinces had a taste for scenes of daily life, such as *Recreation on the Ice* by Hendrick Avercamp (above), *The Meal* by Jan Steen (right), and the etching of *The Skater* by Rembrandt (below).

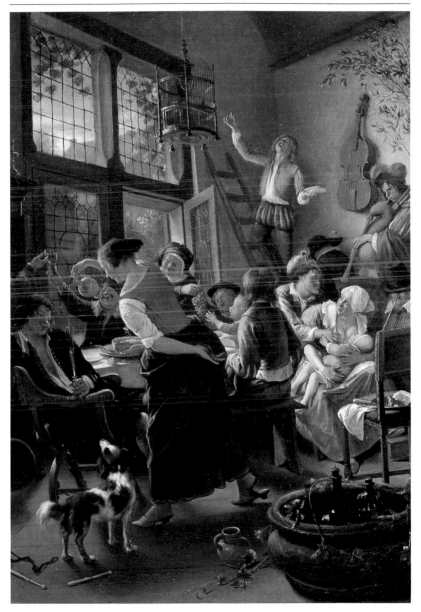

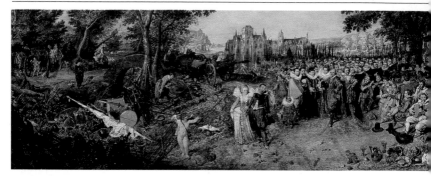

tricks of the buffoons. And when the fun was over there were everyday amusements: dice, or the game of "goose," using counters on a board. Preachers condemned the playing of cards, but cards could be found everywhere, as popular in private houses as in the streets and taverns.

There was time for prayer, too. Not a day went by without readings from the Holy Writ. No meal began without the saying of grace. A blessing accompanied even the most frugal of repasts, *hoosepot*, a dish of boiled meat and vegetables cooked once a week and reheated daily.

In 1616 Adriaen Pietersz van de Venne painted an allegory of the twelve-year truce of 1609 (above). The couple advancing in the middle of the picture symbolizes the United Provinces, recognized and liberated at last, while Discord and Envy have to take refuge behind a tree.

1609: The War Ended at Last

In the name of Spain, Albert the Pious, Archduke of Austria and Governor of the Spanish Netherlands, made a twelve-year truce with the seven provinces that had adopted the Reformation and were represented by Maurice of Nassau of the ruling family of Orange. The United Provinces was free.

Deputies from each of the seven provinces made up the government, which had its headquarters in The Hague. It was headed by the stadtholder, a military leader whose function

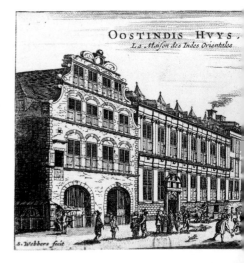

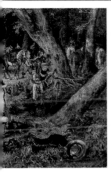

was more to adjudicate than to issue orders. A national figurehead, he had no fiscal or legislative power. The real authority in the United Provinces, the property-owning middle class, was broadly held together by an abiding loyalty to the family of Orange. No one was exempt from tax. Money was the dividing line between the classes.

This plate of Delft china, its blue decoration based on the engravings of Adolf van der Laan, illustrates the packing of herring into barrels. The use of salt to preserve herring, started in the late 14th century, brought prosperity to the ports of the Zuider Zee.

Wealth from Trade

In 1602 the Dutch East India Company was founded. It drew together all the resources of the Netherlands; it owned boats, docks, warehouses, shops, depots. It had a general staff running an army of several thousand men and a sizable navy of vessels. Seven years later the company appointed a governor for overseas territories, and, suddenly, everyone could aspire to a share of the lucrative spice trade.

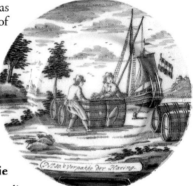

A Prosperous and Puritanical Bourgeoisie

The postal routes of Europe had been channeling financial information into Amsterdam for years. And in 1609 the bank of exchange was founded, confirming the city's status as a money market.

Dominated by the port, the church, and the tavern, the citizens of Holland dreamed above all of the fortunes awaiting them in the East. They had two great preoccupations: their austere Calvinist faith, and their enthusiasm for overseas trade. Their leaders, however, were obsessed by wealth and status.

This was the changed world into which Rembrandt was born, the world he was to paint. No longer were the artist's sitters the regents whose pride, as portrayed by Frans Hals (who was born some twenty-five years before Rembrandt), was barely veiled by a hint of reserve. The men and women featured in the comparably serene light of Jan Vermeer (born some twenty-five years after

With its ornamented gables and innumerable windows, the splendid front of East India Company House, seen in this 17th-century engraving (left), symbolized the newfound status conferred on the United Provinces by foreign trade.

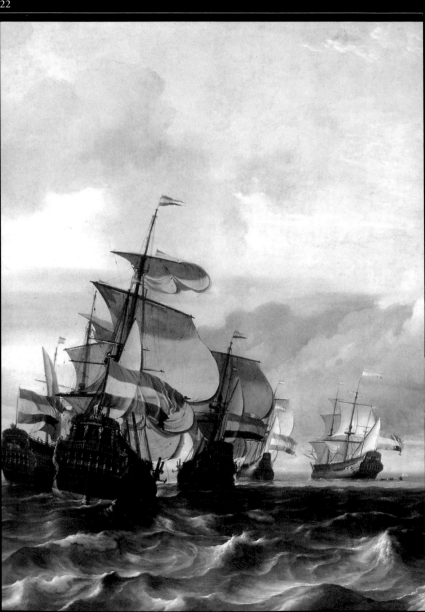

The sailors of northern Holland made a series of expeditions between 1595 and 1600 during which they set up warehouses, notably on the shores of the Indian Ocean. Lured by the promise of huge profits in the spice trade, ships set out in increasing numbers, vying with each other for markets and customers. In 1602 the myriad companies involved joined to form the all-powerful Dutch East India Company. This painting, *The Dutch Fleet of the East India Company*, by Ludolf Backhuysen, was commissioned by the company to commemorate its achievements. The majority of the vessels portrayed, three-masted ships with multiple decks and double forecastles, weighed between six hundred and one thousand tons (an average size, equally suited to transport and piracy).

Rembrandt) were characterized by a delicacy and polish akin to the elegance of the French.

In 1613 Rembrandt Started at the Latin School

There he learned to read and write, in Latin and in Dutch. He read, and reread, the Bible. He must indeed have learned. He entered the University of Leiden at the age of fourteen, not following in the footsteps of his elder brothers, who went to work with their father at a very early age.

However, in 1675, six years after Rembrandt's death, his biographer Joachim von Sandrart claimed that he had scarcely been able to read Dutch and that "books could hardly have been of great help to him" in studying the ancients and the theory of art.

This seems improbable: The University of Leiden is not likely to have admitted a student who could not read. On 20 May 1620, between the names Nicolaus and Gerardus, the university register reads: *Rembrandus hermanni Leydensis studios litterarum annor 14 apud parentes* (Rembrandt Harmensz of Leiden, student of letters, 14 years old, living with his parents).

The University at Which Rembrandt Enrolled to Study the Humanities Was Founded by the State

It had colleges, a library, and lodgings for the students, who were drawn from all over Europe. The teachers were sold accommodation in the Béguinage, usually an almshouse, by the municipality. The university was not bound by any medieval tradition, and the subjects studied included the sciences, Oriental languages, Greek, Latin, astrology, anatomy, and botany—a botanical garden having been created in Leiden in 1587 by Clusius. As an aid to scientific study, the town and its surroundings had been equipped with thermometers, telescopes, and barometers.

Rembrandt spent only a few months at the university. It was enough nevertheless to exempt him from service in the civil guard and the obligation to pay tax on wine and beer, in addition to a number of other privileges. He was not interested in Latin or the study

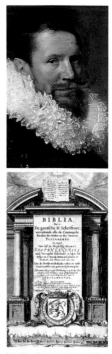

The Dutch painter Frans Hals (1581–1666) belonged to a generation for whom verve was more important than sobriety. This is apparent in his portrait of Paulus van Beresteyn, a judge in Haarlem (detail below).

The frontispiece of the *Statenbijbel* (above), the only version of the Bible recognized by the Calvinist United Provinces. It was published in 1637 in Leiden, a notable printing center.

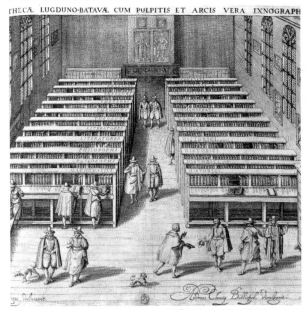

THECA. LUGDUNO-BATAVÆ. CUM PULPITIS ET ARCIS VERA IXNOGRAPH

Founded in 1575, renowned throughout Europe, the University of Leiden is the oldest in Holland. The library, shown in this engraving by Jacob van Swanenburgh (left), was used for study and as a meeting place. It housed the earliest printed works of science and philosophy. Van Swanenburgh also engraved the anatomy theater of the University of Leiden (below). In the early 1600s noted professors were already presenting well-attended anatomy lessons

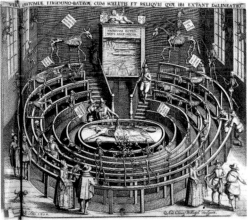

VERA ANATOMIA. LUGDUNO-BATAVÆ. CUM SCELETIS ET RELIQVIS QVÆ IBI EXTANT DELINEATIO

of the *Statenbijbel* (State Bible) prescribed by the Great Synod of Dordrecht in 1618–9 and printed by government order.

In 1641 Johannes Orlers recorded the anxieties of Rembrandt's parents about his education: "As he showed neither taste nor aptitude in this field, his natural bent tending solely to painting and drawing, they found themselves obliged to withdraw their son from the school and decided to place him with a painter so that he could learn the foundations and principles of art. They thus sent him to the master Jacob Isaacsz van Swanenburgh, to whom it fell to instruct and mold him."

Van Swanenburgh Was a Mediocre Painter

Whether one considers his portraits, his architectural views or, for what they are worth, his fantasies, Rembrandt's first master, who worked in the manner of Hieronymus Bosch, was not an outstanding artist. He owed his reputation to a sojourn in Italy, from which he had returned to Leiden in 1617, at the age of forty-six, with a Neapolitan wife, Margherita Cordona.

As in any studio, pupils were taught to pounce wood, prepare a canvas, and grind colors. The apprentice artist had to start by learning the basic procedures. Rembrandt studied the elementary principles of drawing, anatomy, and perspective. In three years he had learned all that van Swanenburgh was able to teach him.

In 1641, the year Johannes Orlers published his guide to Leiden, Rembrandt was still remembered as an excellent student: "He made so much progress that the professionals were left astonished. It was clear that he would one day become an outstanding painter. His father thought the time had come to send him to the highly esteemed painter Pieter Pieterszoon Lastman, who lived in Amsterdam, that he might be given better and more intensive instruction."

Pieter Lastman Was a More Important Influence Than Van Swanenburgh

Like van Swanenburgh, Lastman had spent several years in Italy. He had met Adam Elsheimer in Rome and might also have come across Caravaggio there. In any case he had seen and remembered his work. Lastman painted mythological and biblical subjects. He had no interest in scenes of everyday life such as taverns, village fairs, or guild and corporation banquets; nor did he paint landscapes or still lifes. Lastman

Rembrandt was only twenty in 1626 when he painted *The Angel and the Prophet Balaam* or *Balaam and the Ass* (below), signing it with the monogram RL: L stood for his birthplace, Leiden. His source was clearly Pieter Lastman's painting of the same subject (opposite below), which he would have seen in his master's studio in Amsterdam. He handled his model freely: While the gestures of the prophet on his mount are similar, Rembrandt invests the virtually static pose of Lastman's angel with a flowing sense of movement accentuated by the sweep of the draped clothes.

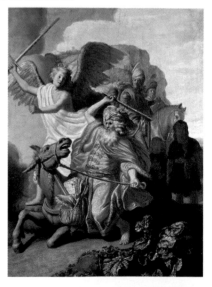

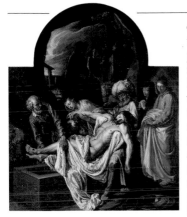

owed his reputation to his history painting. He was forty-one and Rembrandt eighteen when they worked together. In six months Rembrandt mastered Lastman's subject matter and the art of composition. This brief period had a decisive influence on him.

This *Entombment* painted by Pieter Lastman (left) following his return to Holland evokes the work of Caravaggio in its use of light. While he had adopted chiaroscuro (modeling in light and shade), Lastman did not rival Rembrandt in his composition and failed to achieve a truly dramatic effect.

Rembrandt Returned to Leiden Confident of His Abilities

It was a short journey of some twenty-five miles, usually undertaken in a flat-bottomed barge towed along the canal. In Leiden Rembrandt set up his own studio, probably in his father's house on the Weddesteeg. He worked with another painter, Jan Lievens, barely a year

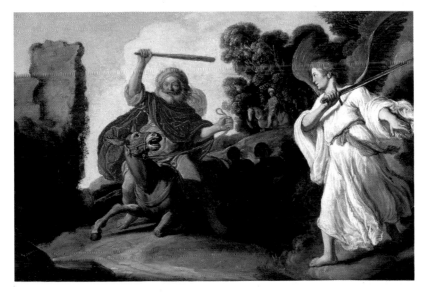

younger than himself. Like Rembrandt, Lievens was
from Leiden and had been one of Lastman's pupils in
Amsterdam. At the age of eight, when Rembrandt was
at the Latin school, Lievens started his apprenticeship
with a Leiden painter, Joris van Schooten. (Might
Rembrandt too have passed through his studio?) He
then moved to Lastman's studio in Amsterdam. By the
time he was eighteen Lievens had had many years of
experience. Now the two artists had only to paint, to
make their names, and to sell.

In Holland a Painter Was Just Another Citizen

Neither church nor state commissioned works of art.
Chapels were bare of paintings and altarpieces. And the
funds at the disposal of the stadtholder were by no
means princely. Artists thus had to obtain their
commissions from their fellow citizens.

These were people who were constantly aware of the
Bible and of their own dignity. They had no desire to be
patrons—they were simply clients whose requirements
the artist had to meet. In particular they expected that a
painting should reflect their sobriety and their ambition.
They wanted to recognize themselves and the spirit that
drove them in a picture.

Jan Lievens and
Rembrandt worked
together in their studio.
While Rembrandt signed
himself RL, Lievens used
the monogram IL in his
Self-Portrait, c. 1635
(detail below). The L
could have referred to his
name or his birthplace.

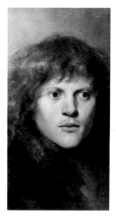

The sea, sky, storm
clouds, and mists
were the natural setting of
life in Holland. Below:
Salomon van Ruysdael's
The Ferry (detail).

The "Miller's Son" Was Talked About

In 1628 Aernout van Buchell, a jurist and broker from Utrecht, visited Leiden and remarked in his *Res pictoriae* that a "miller's son" there was very highly esteemed, adding in Latin "*sed ante tempus*" ("but prematurely"). What painting or paintings might van Buchell have seen to prompt this remark? Perhaps Rembrandt's earliest known work, *The Stoning of St. Stephen*, oil on wood signed and dated "Rf 1625," though

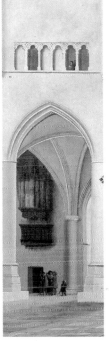

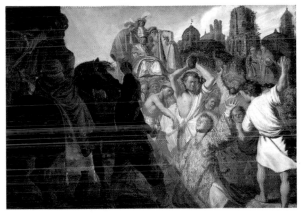

it may already have left the artist's studio by that time.

Other candidates—though again these might have been sold by 1628—would have been *David Presenting the Head of Goliath to Saul, Anna Accused by Tobit of Stealing the Kid*, signed and dated "RH 1626," and *Christ Driving the Moneychangers from the Temple*; also

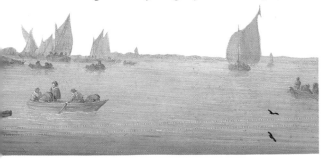

This painting of *The Cathedral of St. Bavo in Haarlem* (detail above) shows an austere interior, bare of frescoes and paintings. It is by Pieter Jansz Saenredam.

In *The Stoning of St. Stephen* (above left) Rembrandt boldly tackled a genre esteemed throughout Europe. Painting meant the portrayal of history, both sacred and profane. The serene face of the saint among the men about to stone him was given Rembrandt's features.

The Music Party, a delightful scene of provincial life in which the artist's brothers and sisters were used as models. Further paintings that could have fueled Rembrandt's rising reputation are *St. Paul in Prison, Two Scholars Disputing, The Flight into Egypt*, and *Samson and Delilah*, painted in 1627. Or was it *The Moneychanger* that van Buchell saw? Or *St. Peter's Denial of Christ*?

Perhaps Rembrandt had hung his portrait of his father on his studio wall—an old man in a dark cap, head bent forward, white beard partly plunged in shadow—or one of his self-portraits, in which the glints in his hair were achieved by exposing the wood underneath (probably by scratching the paint with the handle of the paintbrush).

Rembrandt might also have shown van Buchell his self-portrait *The Artist in His Studio*, the artist standing before an easel, a palette, some paintbrushes, and a painter's rest gripped in his left hand. This is the portrait of his ambition. The wooden panel resting horizontally

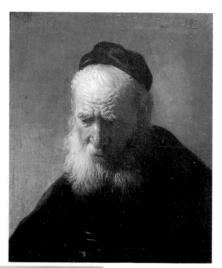

Rembrandt's *Old Man with a White Beard* (1626) was probably his father. The face resembles some of those in *Christ Driving the Moneychangers from the Temple* (right).

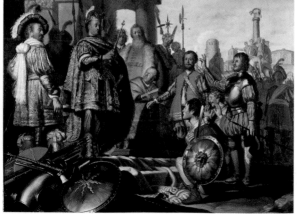

Several titles have been given to Rembrandt's 1626 painting on wood (left): *The Clemency of Titus, The Condemnation of the Son of Manlius Torquatus, The Judgment of Brutus*, and *The Consul Cerialis and the German Legions*. At the age of twenty he was already proving his mastery of history painting and powers of invention. The face partly obscured by the raised scepter is his own.

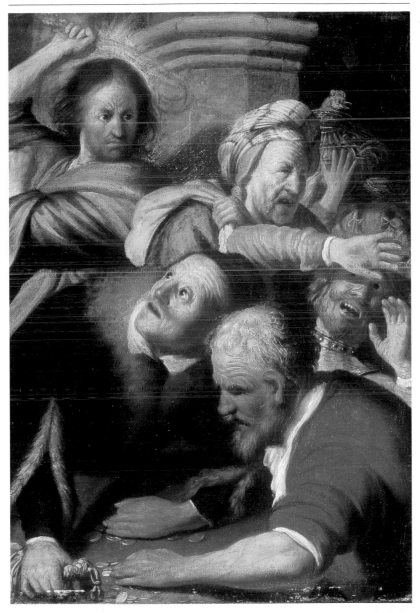

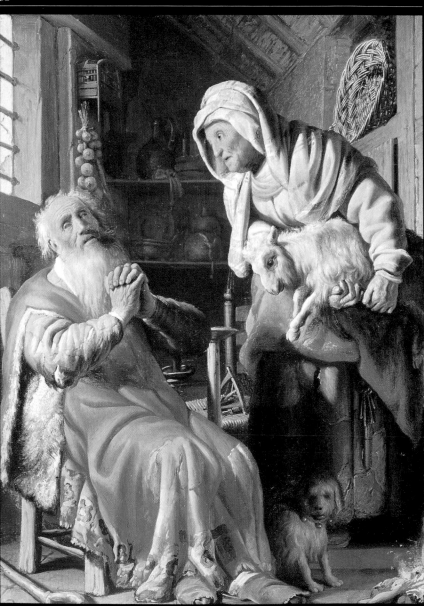

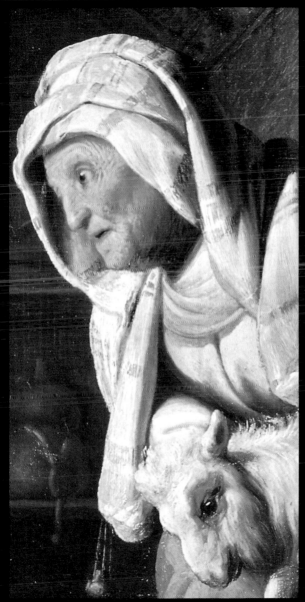

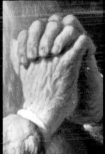

The subject of this painting dating from 1626, *Anna Accused by Tobit of Stealing the Kid*, was taken by Rembrandt from the Bible (Tobit 2:11–14). Tobit, blinded by the hot droppings of sparrows, heard the bleating of an animal brought home by his wife. He called to her and said, "Where does this creature come from? Suppose it has been stolen! Quick, let the owners have it back; we have no right to eat stolen goods." She said, "No, it was a present given me over and above my wages." He did not believe her, and told her to give it back to the owners. Then she answered, "What about your own alms? What about your own good works? Everyone knows what return you have had for them." Tobit sighed and wept and began a prayer of lamentation.

on the easel corresponds in shape and size to Rembrandt's paintings of biblical subjects. And once an artist had mastered these...

In 1626 Rembrandt Began to Etch the Biblical Scenes He Had Already Painted

He etched *The Circumcision* and *The Rest on the Flight into Egypt* that year and *The Flight into Egypt* a year later. Again and again he etched his mother's face and beggars in rags. Was this because wrinkles, stains, and tattered edges could readily be rendered in line and shadow?

In his *Introduction to the Elevated School of Painting* (1678), Rembrandt's student Samuel van Hoogstraten recorded a precept Rembrandt later held up to his pupils: "Make it a rule consciously to practice what you already know; you will then discover that which escapes you and what you wish to learn."

Did Rembrandt himself apply this principle? He was always eager to learn more. For this reason he set out to master the new technique of etching. No doubt he had seen the etchings of Willem Pietersz Buytewech, Esaias van de Velde, Pieter Vinckboons, and Hercules Seghers. No doubt he had begun to buy Jacques Callot's works. Rembrandt was convinced that acid offered greater possibilities as an

Rembrandt did many drawings and etchings of the beggars of Leiden over the years, among them *Beggar in High Cap, Leaning on a Stick* (left), 1629. His etching needle found inspiration in torn clothes and lined faces. The etching of his mother's head (far left) is from 1628.

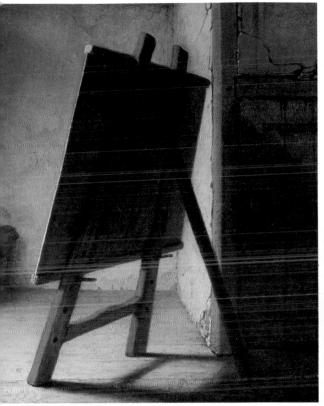

The painter gazing at the panel propped on the easel in full light is Rembrandt himself. Is he contemplating a finished work or a rough sketch? He is not in working apparel but dressed as if to receive clients. This scene, *The Artist in His Studio*, was painted c. 1628.

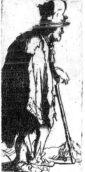

etching tool than the burin (an etcher's steel cutting tool). However, he had to learn to use different varnishes, control the depth of the bite of the acid, and change the etching needles. This required endless practice. He devised a double needle and used it to etch strands of hair.

Rembrandt Was Not Yet Twenty. He Worked and Experimented with Unflagging Energy

In the late 1620s Lievens was probably more highly regarded

Rembrandt was influenced by engravings of other artists, such as Albrecht Dürer. In *Beggar with a Crippled Hand, Leaning on a Stick* (above), he was clearly inspired by the work of Jacques Callot, a French engraver and etcher. An example of Callot's work is *Beggar with a Crutch* (left).

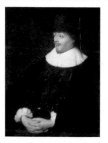

than Rembrandt. It was Lievens who, in about 1626, painted the portrait of Constantijn Huygens (detail left). The latter, some ten years older than the two young artists, was a useful connection. He had served as a diplomat at the embassy of the United Provinces in the Venetian Republic and afterward at the embassy in London, where James I ennobled him. In 1625 Huygens became private secretary to the stadtholder. He translated Latin verse and the poetry of John Donne, studied law, astronomy, and theology, and conducted a correspondence with René Descartes in three languages. He also kept a diary.

Comparing Rembrandt and Lievens

In approximately 1630 Huygens recorded that the "miller's son," Rembrandt, and the "embroiderer's son," Lievens, were already the equals of the most famous painters and would soon surpass them. He went on to draw from their story the moral that the men's humble origins disproved those who claimed their noble blood conferred superiority.

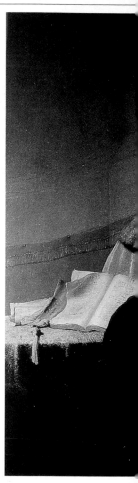

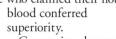

Comparing the two painters to their teachers, Huygens expressed the opinion that they owed them nothing. "If today they could see the work of their pupils, they would feel the same shame as the teachers of Virgil, Cicero, and Archimedes."

Huygens also compared the two men to

Constantijn Huygens commissioned Jan Lievens to paint his portrait (detail above left) c. 1626. He wrote the first critique of Rembrandt's work, remarking on his use of light and shade.

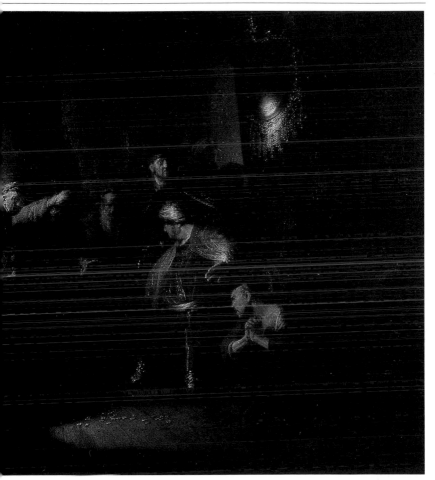

each other: Lievens was superior in invention, while Rembrandt showed greater judgment and more lively emotional expression. Taking the example of *Judas Returning the Thirty Pieces of Silver*, Huygens declared (see pp. 136–7) that the painting surpassed everything that had been produced by antiquity and Italy: An adolescent, son of a miller, had surpassed Protogenes, Apelles, and Parrhasius.

Huygens was impressed by Rembrandt's *Judas Returning the Thirty Pieces of Silver* of 1629 (above). The drawing of two figures (far left) may have been a sketch for the painting.

How Can One Be a Painter in the 17th Century Without Going to Rome?

Huygens was astonished that the two young painters had spent no time in Italy. What 17th-century artist had not visited the country? Poussin, Rubens, Velázquez— the list was endless—had measured their strength in Rome, and the city had continued to serve them as a reference point and a source of models. Neither Lievens nor Rembrandt had thought the journey necessary, for two reasons: because a good number of Italian masterpieces had found their way to Holland and because they lacked the time. The second reason was doubtless the more cogent. Though their attitude surprised Huygens, it was no obstacle to their growing reputation. Robert Ker, the Earl of Ancrum, personal envoy of Charles I of England, visited the United Provinces. Among the works the stadtholder entrusted to him for the king were paintings by Lievens and Rembrandt.

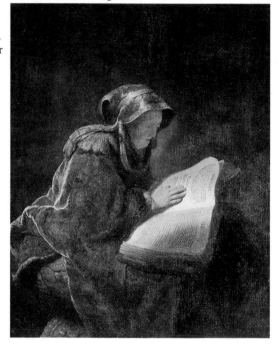

First Pupils, First Sales

Gerrit Dou was the first student to attend Rembrandt's studio. He was then fourteen years old. Huygens' visits to the studio and the advent of pupils were both signs of Rembrandt's growing reputation. Every means of making himself known seemed worth pursuing.

Fifty years after Rembrandt's death the Dutch writer

In 1631, the year he left Leiden, Rembrandt painted *The Prophetess Anna*. Anna had recognized the Child Jesus as the Messiah when he was brought by his parents to the Temple. Did Rembrandt's mother, who posed for this painting, realize her son's genius?

Arnold Houbraken gave the following convincing account: "Every now and then he would be visited by connoisseurs; eventually they recommended that he visit a certain gentleman in The Hague to show him and offer him a newly finished painting. Rembrandt carried the painting to The Hague on foot, and sold it for 100 guilders. This brilliant beginning opened the possibility of wealth up to him, and his enthusiasm for work redoubled, earning him the admiration of all art lovers; now, as the saying goes, he had his hands full of work."

On 23 April 1630 Harmen Gerritsz van Rijn died, at the age of sixty-two. Rembrandt's brothers took charge of the mill. Did the loss of his father mean that Rembrandt had to work harder and sell more? There is no evidence that this was the case.

Fame was his spur. Leiden became constricting. Johannes Orlers recorded: "The successful reception given to his works in 1630 in Amsterdam, where he was often invited to paint portraits and other pictures, led him to move there."

In Leiden most of his portraits had been a preparation for his history paintings, members of his family generally serving as models. Rembrandt's mother had posed for *The Prophetess Anna* and appears as the central figure in *The Presentation of Christ in the Temple*. These portraits were already powerfully expressive and transcended the limitations of what was seen to be a minor genre.

This portrait, *An Old Woman* or *Rembrandt's Mother*, is by Gerrit Dou. He may have copied a now-lost painting by his master. There was frequent overlapping in the work of master and pupils in the studio: To copy was not to "fake," but a way of learning and contributing.

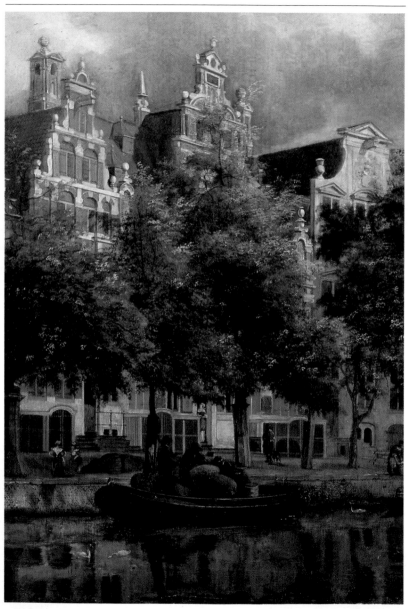

"If it gives us pleasure to see fruit grow in our orchards, do you not think it will give us as much pleasure to see vessels arrive here bringing an abundance of all the produce of India and all that is rare in Europe? What other country could one find in which all the luxuries of life and all the rarities one could desire are so easily available?"

René Descartes

CHAPTER II
REJOICING AND MOURNING

In Jan van der Heyden's painting of *The Herrengracht in Amsterdam* (detail opposite) we see the houses of the well-to-do. Rembrandt's etching *View of Amsterdam* (below) shows the city's port, vessels, windmills, clock towers, and warehouses.

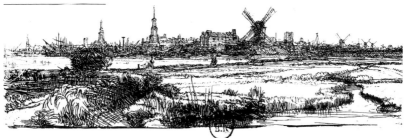

René Descartes, in exile, described the "luxuries" and "rarities" of Amsterdam to his friend the writer Jean Louis Guez de Balzac and observed: "Everyone is so engrossed in furthering his own interests that I could spend the whole of my life here without being noticed by a soul."

Business was indeed thriving. The French writer François de Salignac de la Motte Fénelon later recounted

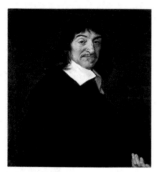

that people came from all over the world to deal, buy, and sell in Amsterdam, whose citizens were "the most eminent merchants in the world." So numerous were the vessels in the harbor that from a distance the masts looked to him like a forest. Three concentric canals, or *grachten*, had been dug in Amsterdam, and these determined the layout of the city. The Westerkerk, the church where Rembrandt would be buried, was finished, and facades of brick and stone were rising all along

The development of Rembrandt's signature reflects his growing ambition.

From the initials, representing his family name and birthplace, of his early years, he moved to signing only his first name—as he moved away from Leiden and his humble beginnings.

the embankments. Amsterdam was a fascinating city brimming with activity, having overtaken Antwerp as the principal port of Holland.

The arrival from Leiden in 1631 of Casparus Barlaeus, professor of philosophy and medicine, was followed by that of other illustrious men, marking the will to establish Amsterdam as a center of creativity, research, and discovery. A university was founded. In the words of the Dutch poet and dramatist Joos van den Vondel, it

The portrait of René Descartes (above left) is after Frans Hals. It testifies to the encounter between a great philosopher and a brilliant portraitist.

was Amsterdam that wore "the crown of Europe," and where "the soul of the state of Holland" resided.

Rembrandt Established Himself in Amsterdam

The young painter was soon signing his works simply "Rembrandt," or occasionally still "R. van Rijn." In the past he had preferred "RHL van Rijn" (R for Rembrandt, H for Harmensz—son of Harmen— and L for Leydensis) or the initials RHL. Now there was no need to go on using the name of his father, who had died in 1630. And why retain the connection with Leiden when he had left it? The quick progression to signing "Rembrandt" followed by "f," "fe," or "ft," representing the Latin *fecit* (made),

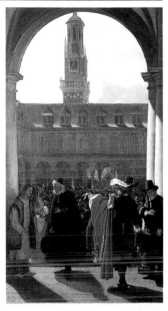

betrays the extent of his ambition. He wanted to be known by his first name alone, like the great Italian masters Titian, Raphael, and Michelangelo. At the age of twenty-seven he saw himself as their equal.

An Important Commission: A Group Portrait of an Anatomy Lesson

For months Rembrandt had been making regular trips from Leiden to work on commissioned portraits. It was probably the Amsterdam art dealer Hendrick van Ulenborch, with whom he had formed a partnership for 1000 guilders (a contract dated 29 June 1631 bears witness), who procured his most prestigious commission. The dealer had only been operating in the city since 1627, having previously lived in Poland and Denmark. He handled works of art from all over Europe,

The Amsterdam stock exchange was built between 1608 and 1611. Trading took place not in the building itself but in the courtyard, the arcades providing shelter when it rained. *The Courtyard of the Old Exchange, Amsterdam* (detail above), dated 1653, is by the Dutch painter Emanuel de Witte. This artist had recently moved to Amsterdam, where he concentrated on architectural paintings.

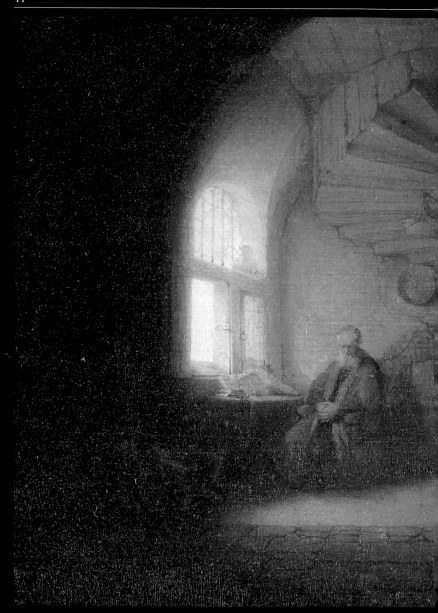

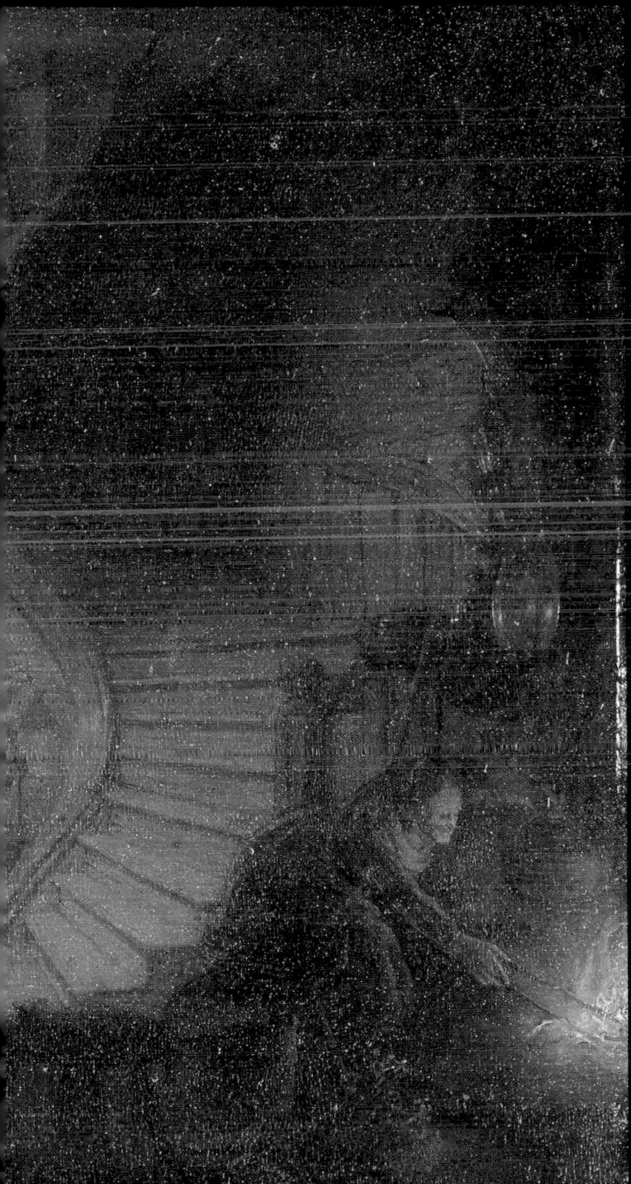

"The spiral of a winding
stair descending from the
shadows and the glimpse
of a deserted gallery
imperceptibly give the
viewer the impression
that he is examining
the interior of a strange
shell inhabited by a little
intellectual animal who
has secreted the luminous
substance. The idea of
withdrawal into oneself,
of depths, of a richness
of understanding born
within the individual
self, are suggested by
this composition,
which in some vague,
inexpressible way, has
a spiritual content."
Paul Valéry,
*The Return from Holland:
Descartes and Rembrandt,*
1926

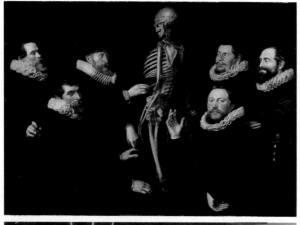

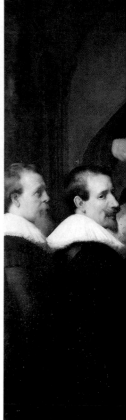

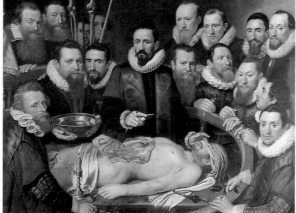

particularly from Italy. Convinced of Rembrandt's talent, he guaranteed him room and board and also provided him with a studio in his own house. He encouraged Rembrandt to rank himself alongside the great masters.

The prestigious commission was to paint an anatomy lesson (using the corpse of a criminal sentenced to death) given in January 1632 by the forty-year-old Professor Nicolaas Pieterszoon Tulp. The painting was probably to mark the first anniversary of the lessons given by the

The artistic tradition of anatomy lessons went back a hundred years. Typical were paintings of the anatomy lessons of Dr. Sebastian Egbertsz by Thomas de Keyser (top left) and of Dr. van der Meer by Pieter Michelsz van Miereveld (above left).

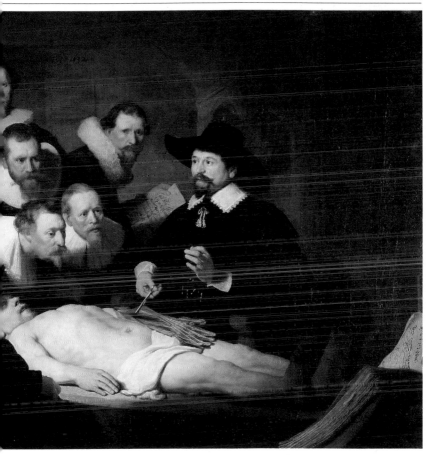

professor in the anatomical theater of the
Anthoniesmarkt. The finished work was to hang
in one of the guild halls. This place was significant
for Rembrandt, as only people of note frequented it,
Tulp being one of them. A well-known surgeon, he
had twice been elected burgomaster of the town
and remained a magistrate. This was the man
Rembrandt was commissioned to paint, depicted in
the company of other illustrious men, none of whom
was a surgeon.

In Rembrandt's *The Anatomy Lesson of Professor Tulp* (above) the worthies around Tulp are not doctors. The list held by the man in the center bears the names of government officials—but the man the picture immortalized was the artist himself.

Rembrandt Knew His *Anatomy Lesson* Would Invite Comparisons and Be Crucial to His Career

If approved and admired, the work would lead to a brilliant future. What Rembrandt had to do was to astonish and yet win acceptance, to startle the viewer, while respecting the solemnity of the occasion.

Group portraits had been popular in Holland for over a century. *The Anatomy Lesson of Professor Tulp* thus had both to respect tradition and stand out from the rest.

The conventional group portrait presented its sitters in a formal pose in even light. Whether they were around a banquet or council table or in an anatomy theater made little difference to the manner in which they were portrayed. Their attitudes remained stiff, and they seemed virtually indifferent to the occasion. By contrast, the men around Tulp seem to be genuinely attending an anatomy lesson. They bend over the corpse in silent concentration, examining the exposed tendons of the

There was a sculpted tulip on the front of the house of the *praefector anatomiae*, Professor Tulp (portrait below, detail). His name is Dutch for tulip, the flower that is something of a national emblem. Appointed magistrate in 1622 and twice elected burgomaster, Tulp was an established figure in Amsterdam society. Rembrandt probably studied the plates in *De humani corporis fabrica*, 1543, by Andreas Vesalius, the celebrated Flemish anatomist and friend of Titian, in preparation for this work.

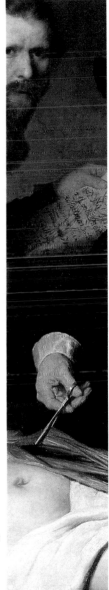

dissected arm. Rembrandt was aware that the men posing for him wanted all who saw the portrait to appreciate their importance and learning. The dominant figure in the group is thus used, by the significant look in his eyes, to convey a sense of moment.

The Painting Astonished Rembrandt's Clients, and It Won Him Instant Renown

On 26 July 1632 Rembrandt received a visit from a bailiff who had been sent by men who had laid wagers on the health of various celebrities in Amsterdam. Rembrandt finally numbered among the famous.

Soon after this, Rembrandt met a relative of the art dealer Hendrick van Ulenborch, with whom he lived on the corner of Zwanenburgwal and Sint Anthonies-breestraat. She came from Friesland, where her father had been burgomaster of Leeuwarden. Her name was Saskia. This young woman with rounded chin and full breasts was an orphan. Her father had died in 1624 when she was twelve. She was the youngest of her family—which did not preclude her having a dowry of 40,000 guilders. Unusually for a girl in those days, she knew how to read and write.

On 5 June 1633 Rembrandt and Saskia Became Engaged

Rembrandt drew Saskia's portrait shadowed by the brim of a flowered hat. Under the line of the edge of the table on which she rests her elbows, a smile on her lips and a flower in her hand, Rembrandt wrote: "Portrait of my wife when she was twenty-one years old, the third day after we were betrothed." Like his father and mother, Saskia became Rembrandt's model.

A year to the day after their betrothal Rembrandt and Saskia's guardian, the preacher Jan Cornelisz Sylvius, went to the commissioners in Amsterdam to arrange the marriage. Rembrandt had still to obtain his mother's consent; an assenting note was added later in the margin, having been registered before a notary in Leiden. The couple left for Friesland, in the northern Netherlands, and on 22 June 1634 Rembrandt and Saskia were married. A few weeks earlier, in the album of a German merchant

staying with Hendrick van Ulenborch, Rembrandt had written: "An upright man respects honor before wealth." He could well afford such sentiments, given Saskia's dowry and the influx of commissions at the time.

Rembrandt Harmensz van Rijn, son of a miller from Leiden, now had lawyers and an officer as his brothers-in-law. One of his sisters-in-law, Hiskje, had married the prosperous Gerrit van Loo. Marriage radically altered Rembrandt's social status: "The miller's son" was a man of the past.

Rembrandt's first portrait of Saskia, as his betrothed (above). Docile, almost resigned in her expression of good humor, did Saskia realize, as she sat for *Saskia Smiling with a Plumed Beret* (right), that she was embarking on a career as a model?

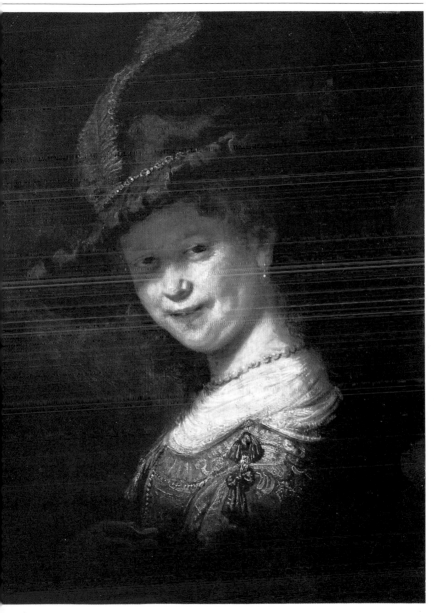

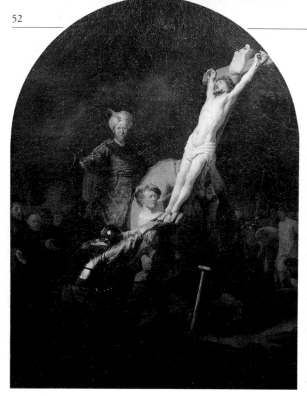

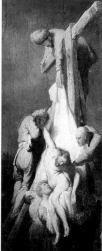

Rembrandt in Love, Rich, and Famous

He received a commission from the stadtholder himself. A year later he wrote to Constantijn Huygens, who had doubtless obtained it for him:

"My dear Sir and most gracious Mr. Huygens, I hope your lordship will be so kind as to advise His Excellency that I am very diligently engaged in proficiently completing the three Passion pictures which His Excellency has personally commissioned me [to do]: an Entombment, a Resurrection, and an Ascension of Christ. These are companion pictures to Christ's Elevation [*The Raising of the Cross*] and His Descent from the Cross. Of these above three, one has been completed, namely Christ's Ascension to Heaven, and the other two are more than half-finished.

The light in *The Raising of the Cross* (above left) falls diagonally along the line traced by the figures of Christ and the soldier raising the cross. Like *The Descent from the Cross* (detail above), this was one of five paintings commissioned from Rembrandt in 1634 by the stadtholder of the United Provinces, Frederick Henry. The common theme was the Passion of Christ.

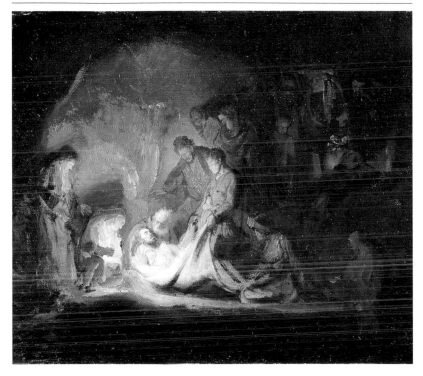

"Please, Sir, let me know whether it would please His Excellency to have the finished piece first, or all three together, so that I may best serve His Excellency the Prince, according to his desires. As a token of my readiness to serve you with my favor, I cannot refrain from presenting to you, dear Sir, my latest work. I trust that you will most graciously accept it in addition to my greetings. I command your lordship and all of yours to God and health. Your obliging and affectionate servant, Rembrandt."

Anxious to receive some payment for the work he had already done, he added the postscript: "I reside next door to the pensionary Boereel on Niuwe [sic] Doelstraat." Saskia and Rembrandt had spent two years with van Ulenborch near the Amstel Canal. Now they needed more space.

Because it is monochrome, *The Entombment*, probably painted in 1639, is thought by some experts to be a sketch for one of Rembrandt's paintings for the stadtholder. The form of the five canvases supplied supports this hypothesis: The upper edge of each has the same arc.

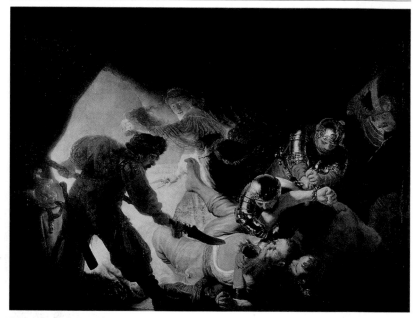

Master and Pupils

Rembrandt now had more pupils. Among them were
Ferdinand Bol, Govaert Flinck, Jacob Adriaensz Backer,
and Gerbrand van den Eekhout. Some of them had to
be provided with a place to live. Painting, etching, and
the teaching of painting and etching required space.
In 1635 he set up a studio in a vast old warehouse over-
looking the Bloemgracht. In the same year Saskia
became pregnant for the first time. Rumbartus was
born and baptized in December, but he lived only
two months.

Rembrandt painted, drew, and etched. He taught
his pupils to measure the proportions of a body, to ink
a copperplate, and to grind colors. He made love to
Saskia, drank beer and gin, and frequented the auction
rooms. Rembrandt wanted everything: to have
everything and to understand everything.

He studied works he would never see and sketched
towns he would never visit. He copied Leonardo da

Rembrandt gave *The
Blinding of Samson*
(above) to Constantijn
Huygens to thank him
for procuring
commissions from the
stadtholder. It is a
violent scene, which,
in the harshness of
its composition,
brings Rembrandt
close to a tradition
of Italian art.

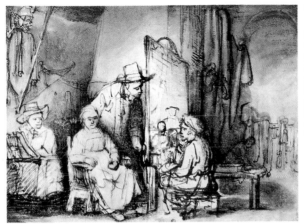

Whether by Rembrandt or one of his pupils, the drawing of *The Studio* (left) is a vivid rendering of what went on there: The painter is at work with the model, one pupil is grinding colors, and another is sketching or reading.

Vinci's *Last Supper* and drew views of London and Italian landscapes. He needed to dream dreams, as he needed to study his surroundings, to observe Saskia's pose with a child in her arms, and to scrutinize the heavy trudge of a couple of peasants or the posture of a woman making pancakes. Wearying of the unrelieved severity of his commissioned portraits—

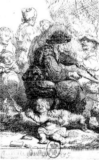

Rembrandt covered all manner of subjects in his studio, ranging from *The Pancake Woman* in the street (above) to a *Mother Nursing Her Child* (left), in this case drawn by one of his pupils, Ferdinand Bol.

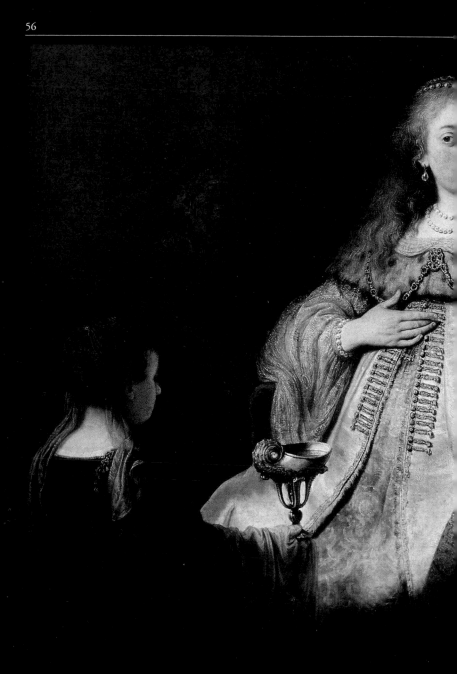

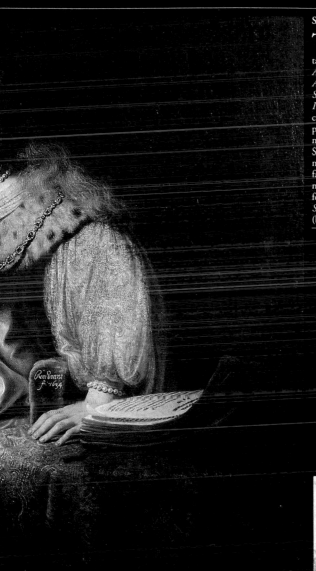

Saskia, Model of Love

T his painting by
Rembrandt has been
taken variously to be
*Artemisia Receiving the
Ashes of Mausolus* or
*Sophonisba Receiving the
Poisoned Cup.* In either
case the subject of the
painting touches on
marital fidelity, and
Saskia, present in so
many of Rembrandt's
fantasies, served as the
model. She is also
featured in Rembrandt's
Self-Portrait with Saskia
(below) of 1636.

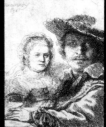

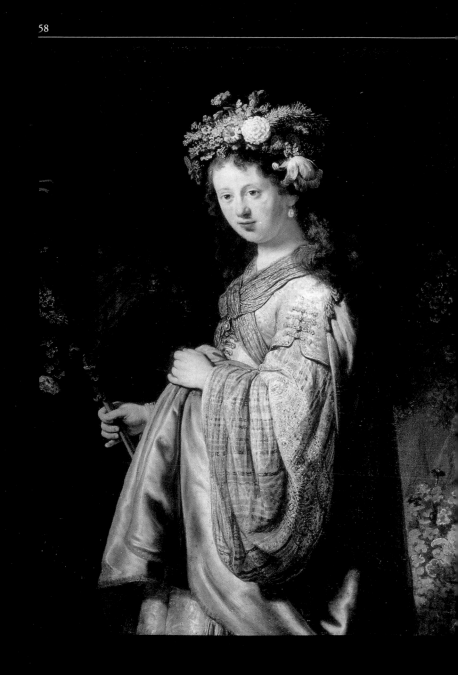

Goddess and Woman

Rembrandt did not confine himself to straightforward portraits of Saskia. She appeared in many guises in his paintings. In *Saskia as Flora* (opposite) she is the goddess of the Italian countryside. Possibly someone had mentioned to Rembrandt that prostitutes in Rome invoked the protection of Flora, but the portrait's sensuality speaks for itself. The artist gives his Roman goddess a Dutch flavor by slipping a tulip into her floral wreath. In the *Portrait of Saskia van Ulenborch* (detail left) Rembrandt presents her as elegant, her hat betraying an awareness of French fashions. Both paintings date from 1634.

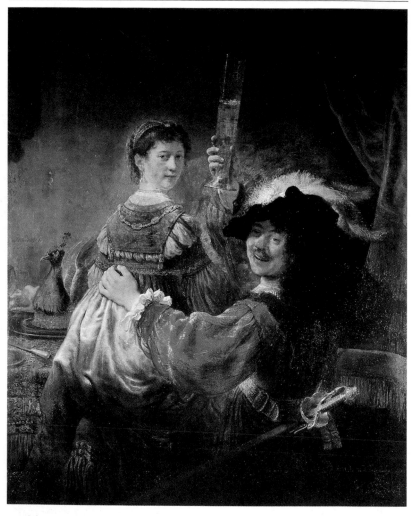

models attired in black set off by lace collars or ruffs—he decked old men out in turbans, robes, and weapons and used them as models. He bought scimitars, brocades, and silks for these portraits, as well as engravings and canvases to copy. Saskia's family grew worried by his extravagance and accused Rembrandt of squandering his

Rembrandt's *Self-Portrait with Saskia* (1636) was his reply to those detractors who accused him of wasting his wife's dowry. He raises his glass to them.

wife's dowry. Rembrandt retorted that he was rich and that was the end of it. Who could deny it?

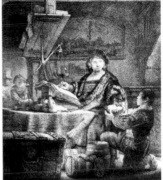

Jan Uytenbogaert, the Receiver-General or *The Goldweigher*, 1639.

The Impatient Rembrandt

Even the stadtholder owed him money, as he had no hesitation in reporting to Constantijn Huygens in a letter written "in haste this 27 January 1639." He told him that the tax collector Jan Uytenbogaert had called while he was wrapping two works for the stadtholder and added: "He mentioned that if it pleased His Highness, he was prepared to make payments to me from his office here. Therefore, may I ask you, my dear Sir, that the money which His Highness allows me for these two pieces be paid here as soon as possible, because I could use it well, particularly at the present time." A few weeks passed. Rembrandt grew impatient: "My dear Sir, I hesitate to trouble you with this letter, but I am doing so because of what Uytenbogaert, the tax collector, told me after I complained to him about the delay in my payment. Volbergen, the treasurer, denied that dues were claimed annually. Last Wednesday, Uytenbogaert, the collector, replied to this that Volbergen had thus far laid claim to these dues every six months, so that more than 4000…guilders had been deposited again at his office. And because of this true state of affairs, I beg you, kind Sir, to have my payment order prepared promptly, so that I will

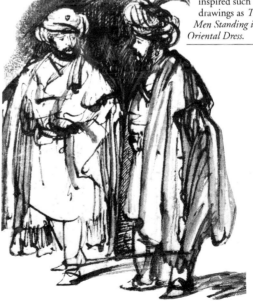

*R*embrandt, a collector, owned a few Indian miniatures, which inspired such drawings as *Two Men Standing in Oriental Dress*.

now finally receive my well-earned 1244 guilders."

This sum was twice the 600 guilders Rembrandt had reluctantly agreed to for each canvas—less than he might have hoped—plus 44 guilders to cover the cost of the ebony frame and the packing. Rembrandt again gave his address: "I reside on the Binnen Amstel. The house is called the sugar bakery." This shop, De Vier Suykerbrooden, where he had lived for several weeks, belonged to a Jan van Veldestijn. It was not to be his last address.

Rembrandt Wanted an Address Worthy of His Reputation

While waiting impatiently for the sum owed to him by the stadtholder, Rembrandt negotiated the purchase of a house built in 1606 in the prosperous area of Sint Anthoniesdijk on the Breestraat, often known as Sint Anthoniesbreestraat. The house had two principal floors topped by a stepped gable. The owners, Pieter Belten and Christoffel Thijsz, demanded a price of 13,000 guilders, not all payable at once. The contract of sale stipulated that Rembrandt must pay a quarter of the amount in three installments in the first year. The balance was to be paid in five or six years. Any amount outstanding would then incur interest of five percent. On 1 May 1639 Rembrandt and Saskia moved to their new address. It was next door to the dealer van Ulenborch, in whose house they had met.

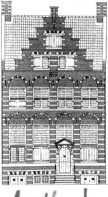

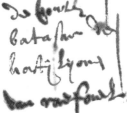

T his engraving shows the house on Sint Anthoniesbreestraat as Rembrandt would have known it.

Rembrandt, Reproached for Never Having Been to Italy, Discovered Italian Art in Amsterdam

It was doubtless because he was raising money for the house that Rembrandt failed to outbid a competitor on 9 April. That day Raphael's *Portrait of Baldassare Castiglione* was auctioned at the house of the dealer Lucas van Uffelen.

During the sale he drew a portrait, noting upon the drawing the selling price of the Raphael, 3500 guilders. The purchaser was Alphonso Lopez, a Spanish diamond and picture dealer living on the Singelgracht in Amsterdam. He supplied the French court and Cardinal Richelieu, patron of the arts and founder of the French

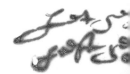

Academy, with works of art. In his collection Rembrandt saw a portrait by another Italian master, Titian's *Ariosto*. Lopez also owned a Rembrandt, *Balaam and the Ass*, signed and dated "RL 1626." Rembrandt copied Raphael and Titian, rendering the poses of Baldassare Castiglione and Ariosto in his own manner. It is often from paintings that paintings are born.

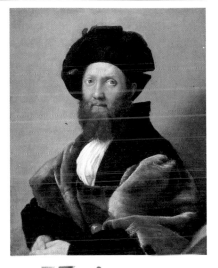

Raphael's *Portrait of Baldassare Castiglione*, dated 1516 (above), was copied by Rembrandt in a 1639 self-portrait (left).

Rembrandt painted relentlessly in his house on Sint Anthoniesbreestraat. His studio was upstairs, above the family living quarters. Pictures and portfolios of etchings began to accumulate in one of the adjacent rooms; the other was filled with weapons, exotic garments, and curios. On the very top floor were more studios, used by Rembrandt's pupils. There they prepared the mixture of bitumen, beeswax, and resin that was used to coat the copperplates, or they made copies of Rembrandt's paintings, which he himself altered and reworked.

As to the fate of those pictures that were neither copies nor originals, no one was much concerned. Authenticity was not an issue. What mattered was to paint.

Cornelia, a Name To Mourn, and a Time of Sadness

A second baby, Cornelia, was baptized in July 1638, but she died three weeks later. Then, at the end of 1639, Saskia became pregnant for the third time. Hope rose anew.

The daughter, born in July 1640 and also given the name Cornelia, survived only two weeks. Her death was followed by that of Rembrandt's mother, Cornelia, in Leiden. She left an inheritance of 9160 guilders. A few months afterward

A handwritten note identifies this drawing as "Rembrandt in the clothes he normally wore when painting."

Titia, the sister to whom Saskia had probably been closest, died in her turn.

The still life of a flayed ox painted in Rembrandt's studio early in 1640 is ultimately a religious picture. The dead meat was a comment on the fragility of human life, far removed from the flesh of the elegant models Rembrandt was painting at the same period. Did any of Rembrandt's contemporaries understand?

Despite his grief, Rembrandt continued to work. An Englishman called Peter Mundy who passed through Amsterdam mentioned the name of only one Dutch painter in his travel diary, and that was Rembrandt. Johannes Orlers added a note about him in the second edition of his *Description of the Town of Leiden,* published in 1641.

Rembrandt's name also attracted a mention in Tommaso Garzoni's *Piazza Universale,* published in Basel by Matthaus Merian.

Like Jacques Callot and Abraham Bosse, he was one of the recognized masters of etching in the 17th century. Rembrandt's fame as a painter and etcher was spreading throughout Europe. The French painter Claude Vignon had seen *Balaam and the Ass,* owned by Alphonso Lopez, and thought highly of it. He sent his respects to Rembrandt and advised a traveling friend of his, an art dealer, to bring back some of Rembrandt's work from Amsterdam.

The authenticity of this *Flayed Ox* (1640), strikingly three-dimensional, is doubted by some experts.

The Power of Rembrandt's Portraits: Exactly What the Patrons Wanted

Rembrandt was greatly admired. even adulated. But he was not content just to be a fashionable painter. He had portrayed Marten Soolmans and his wife, Oepjen Coppit, in all their splendor—their gloves, their lace and finery—in 1634; he had painted the ruffs of the merchant Willem Burchgraeff and his wife, Margaretha Bilderbeeck; he had painted a shipowner, his hand resting on a drawing of a ship, while his wife is delivering him a note. These were "functional" portraits, which were exactly what their patrons wanted.

When in 1640 he painted a pair of portraits of Herman Doomer, framer and gilder, and his wife, Baartjen Martens, he harked back to the earlier depictions of Jan Cornelisz Sylvius and Jan Uytenbogaert. These portraits are not renderings of the status and

M ennonite preacher and prosperous merchant Cornelis Claesz Anslo is the subject of these three portraits by Rembrandt: a drawing (left), a painting (above), and an etching (opposite).

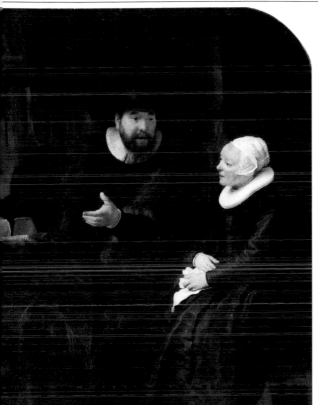

R embrandt often arrived at a painting by careful and unhurried preparatory work. For example, in 1640 he drew a portrait of Anslo. In 1641 he developed this into an etching, which more precisely rendered the face. The poet Joos van den Vondel wrote: "Rembrandt really needs to paint Cornelis' voice. His external appearance is what is least representative of him, and what is invisible can only be known by sound: Whoever wants to see Anslo should listen to him." Rembrandt met the challenge. Does not the raised hand gesturing to the open book in front of him (below) make his voice audible? The same year (1641) Rembrandt painted another portrait of Anslo (left), his hand raised in the direction of a woman who is listening to him.

Cornelis Claesz Anslo

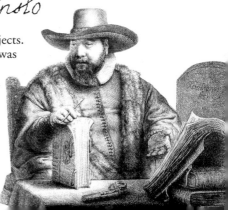

role of the sitter, but musings on his subjects. In this painting of Doomer Rembrandt was also undoubtedly trying to recapture the intensity that marks his then-unfinished painting of Cornelis Claesz Anslo. In it, Anslo appears at a table piled with books, talking to a woman sitting next to him. Sylvius, Uytenbogaert, and Anslo are all shown with the Bible and preaching. The first was a Calvinist,

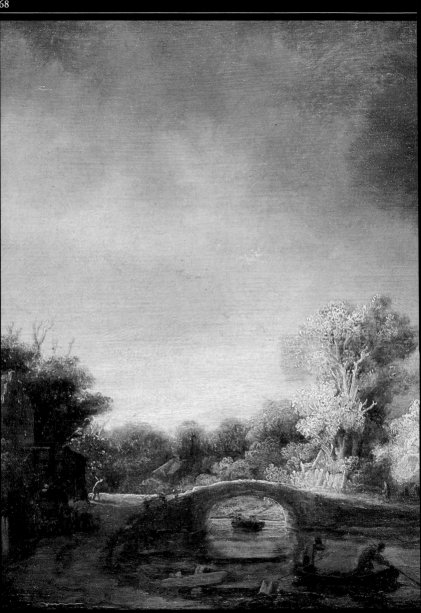

Rembrandt's landscapes are far removed from those of the golden age of Dutch painting, which, while smooth and spilling over with light, are for the most part only the setting for an incident or episode. Rembrandt painted myths. The elements he carefully selects from ordinary life tell a story of their own. For example, this *Landscape with a Stone Bridge* (1637) features a tavern on the left and a church tower on the right, symbols of the two poles between which life in 17th-century Holland was lived.

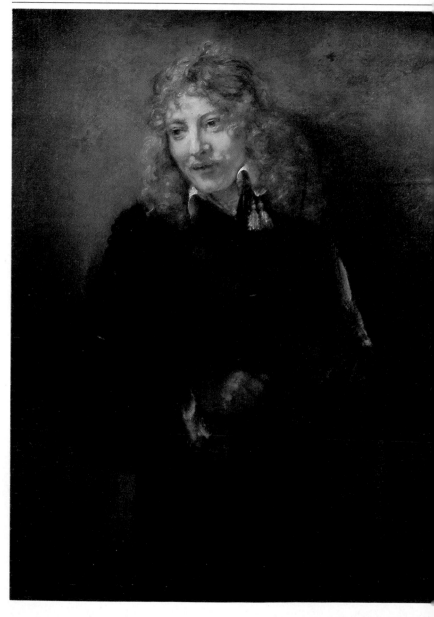

the second a member of the
Armenian Church, the third
a Mennonite. These works of
Rembrandt are meditations
on the words of the apostles
and the prophets.

Chiaroscuro: Light and Dark

In order to paint dreams,
meditations, and thoughts,
Rembrandt created a wholly
new way of using light. The
external world was no longer
his subject.

He bought prints all the
time and through them
studied Italian art. Being
black and white, they
disclosed nothing of the
brilliance of the original
canvases and frescoes or of
the materials used. All

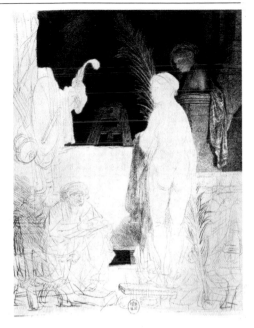

they revealed was the composition of a work and the
arrangement and play of light and shadow.

From his experience with copperplate etching
Rembrandt knew the lines to cut with the etcher's
needle and the depth of bite necessary to create shadow.
His understanding of paintings he had never seen in
terms of line and shadow and his extensive practical
experience in etching had a very decisive influence on
his work.

It was not painting but etching that inspired him
when he began to organize light and shadow on his
canvases. Rembrandt used chiaroscuro as if he were
applying ink to paper. By adding color he gave it a
further dimension. This chiaroscuro was not a placing
of shadow where light would logically cast it. It was a
way of providing emphasis in a picture, of creating the
effect the artist desired. If Rembrandt lit a hand and a
glove that should, properly speaking, have been
shadowed by a shoulder, this was because that hand and

The above work,
*The Artist Drawing
from a Model* (1639),
shows a studio crowded
with implements,
objects, and ornaments.

The light that
illuminates the
face of Nicolaes
Bruyningh (opposite)
and cuts across his cuff
and hand demonstrates
the quintessence of
chiaroscuro. The
forcefulness of the
portrait is Rembrandt's
one object, and his firm
control of light, the
secret of its power.

glove had a significance in the painting above and beyond being simple representations.

Over the years Rembrandt abandoned the use of chiaroscuro to achieve dramatic effect. He simultaneously gave up signaling particular details to indicate particular episodes in the Bible. It was enough for him that the arbitrary use of chiaroscuro should serve only the ends of the painting itself.

Rembrandt and Saskia's Attention Was Given to a New Child and a New Commission

On 22 September 1641, at the Zuiderkerk, the fourth child of Saskia and Rembrandt was baptized. He was given the name Titus. Anxious weeks went by, but Titus did not die.

Meanwhile, the ambitious Frans Banning Cocq had become a prominent Amsterdam personality. His marriage to the

The figure with his hand on his hip is Frans Banning Cocq (1605–55). Thanks to his marriage, he became very rich and acquired, in addition to a number of properties, the title of Lord of Purmerland. He was later ennobled by James II. This portrait of him is a detail taken from *The Governors of the Honorable Archers' Guild in Amsterdam* by Bartholomeus van der Helst. Executed over ten years after Rembrandt's *The Night Watch*, it was no doubt exactly what Cocq wanted, presenting him elegantly posed, surrounded by works of art.

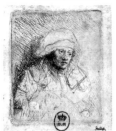

burgomaster's daughter had provided him with the means to fulfill his ambitions. He had quickly become part of the city hierarchy and served a term as burgomaster. He and his wife inhabited one of the finest buildings on the Singelgracht, designed by the architect Hendrick de Keyser.

Cocq's military career had been no less successful and could not pass unsung. He and other militia officers had defended the towns and founded the republic. They had won lasting prestige. When war was no longer waged on Dutch soil—only at sea—the militia and the civil guard had little to do but parade and take part in shooting competitions. So, at the end of 1640 Frans Banning Cocq and the officers of his company commissioned Rembrandt to paint their group portrait, which was completed in 1642.

In the meantime Saskia was making a poor recovery from Titus' birth.

The Portrait of the Company Was to Be Compared to Others

Group portraits of the militia belonged to a tradition longer even than that of anatomy lessons. Once again, Rembrandt's painting had to surpass the works of his predecessors—and also outshine the portraits commissioned by five other companies: the company of Captain Cornelis Bicker, painted by Joachim von Sandrart; the company of Captain Bas, by Govaert Flinck (a former pupil); the company of Captain Roelof Bicker, by Bartholomeus van der Helst; the company of Captain van Vlooswijck, by Nicolaes Eliasz Pickenoy; and that of Captain De Graeff, by Jacob Adriaensz Backer (another of his pupils).

Rembrandt had painted, drawn, and etched Saskia in many guises, smiling, compliant, patient, triumphant. Then in 1641 he etched *Saskia Ill, with Large White Headdress* (above left), portraying her in a state of utter exhaustion, her rounded cheeks sunken, her eyes fixed on empty space. Was it premonition that in 1639 had led Rembrandt to etch *Youth Surprised by Death* and *The Death of the Virgin*, realized after sketches of *Saskia Lying Ill in Bed* (detail above)?

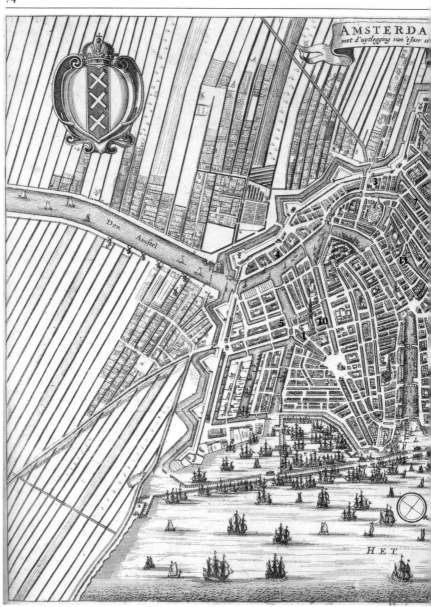

AMSTERDA
met d'uytlegging van 't Jaer 16

Den Amstel

HET

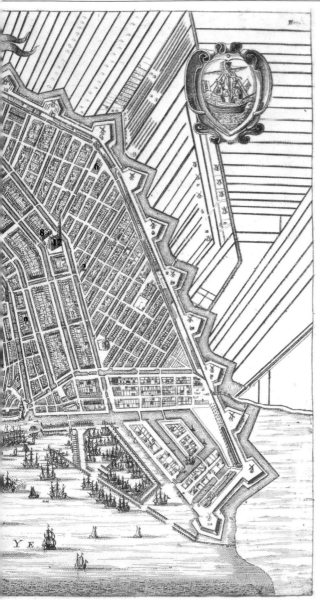

Map of Rembrandt's Amsterdam:

1. House of the painter Pieter Lastman, under whom Rembrandt studied in 1624

2. House on the Doelstraat, where Rembrandt lived with Saskia until 1636

3. The Bloemgracht, where Rembrandt set up a studio in 1635

4. District of Binnen Amstel, where Rembrandt lived until 1639

5. House in Sint Anthoniesdijk on the Breestraat. Bought by Rembrandt and Saskia in 1639, and sold at auction in 1658

6. House on the Rozengracht, where Rembrandt spent the last ten years of his life

7. House inhabited by Titus on the Singelgracht after his marriage to Magdalena van Loo

8. House of Professor Tulp on the Keizersgracht

9. House of Captain Cocq on the Singelgracht

10. Probably Jan Six' residence on the Kloveniersburgwal

11. Keizerskroon Inn, where all of Rembrandt's possessions were sold at auction

12. The Westerkerk, the church where Rembrandt and his family were buried

Saskia was utterly exhausted.

Rembrandt was to receive 1600 guilders for his painting. Each of the sixteen guards paid around 100 guilders, depending on the place he occupied in the composition. It was not a very large sum for a group portrait. Indeed, much more had been paid in Holland for a tulip bulb. It is possible of course that the officers paid a supplement not mentioned in the contract.

Saskia stayed in bed, ill.

Rembrandt Devoted Himself Entirely to the Painting for Weeks, Then Months

Very early in the year 1642 the portrait was delivered. The title of the work, as inscribed in a sketchbook containing a watercolor reproduction, was *The Young Heer van Purmerandt* [Banning Cocq] *as Captain, Ordering His Lieutenant, the Heer van Vlaerdingen* [Willem van Ruytenburch], *to March the Company Out.*

Twelve years after Rembrandt's death Filippo Baldinucci wrote: "He won greater renown than any practitioner of this art. The reason was that among the figures shown a captain had one foot lifted as if in mid-step, and held in his hand a halberd in such well-drawn perspective that...it looked to everybody as if it were lifesize; the other figures, it is true, were mixed and mingled in such a fashion that it was difficult readily to distinguish one from another, however carefully they might have been painted from life."

On 5 June 1642 Saskia Drew Up Her Last Will and Testament

Saskia left approximately 40,000 guilders to Rembrandt and Titus. Half was to revert to Titus. Rembrandt had a life interest until his son came of age or married. But this clause would become null and void if Rembrandt remarried. Saskia did not require Rembrandt to draw up an inventory of his assets and, in a final clause, she

In 1715 Rembrandt's painting *The Company of Captain Frans Banning Cocq* (opposite) was cut down so that it could hang on the second floor of the Nieuwe Stadhuis, later to become the Royal Palace. Roughly ten inches were removed from the top, six inches from the bottom, twelve inches from the left, and four inches from the right: The painting had to fit on the wall between two doors.

Rembrandt exorcised his grief and anxiety by giving them artistic expression. Below: *Saskia Lying Ill in Bed.*

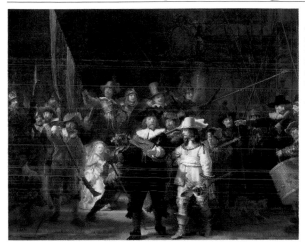

As dust and the ravages of age darkened its tones, Rembrandt's painting of Captain Cocq's company (left) came to be known as *The Night Watch.*

appointed Rembrandt sole guardian of Titus and refused to let Titus' affairs be run by the Court of Orphans.

On 14 June Saskia died, probably from tuberculosis. She was thirty years old. Five days later she was buried. On 9 July her remains were taken to the Oudekerk, a church where Rembrandt had bought a tomb. Titus was barely a year old. Commissions were pouring in from all directions.

In 1642 *The Company of Captain Frans Banning Cocq* brought Rembrandt growing renown, while his private life fell to pieces with Saskia's death.

Is *The Sick Man of Samaria* (below) attended by doctors, not, in fact, a dying woman?

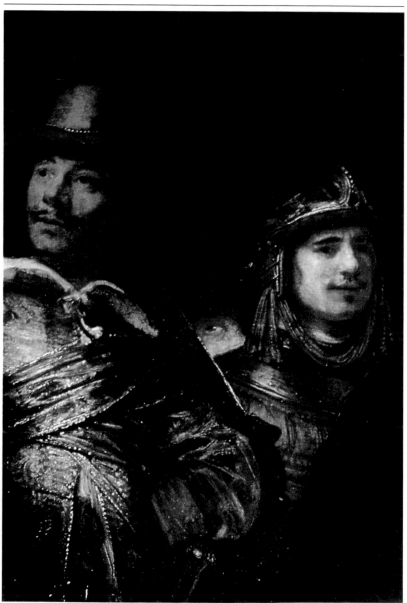

"This painting, whatever the criticisms of it may be, will survive all its competitors because it is so painterly in conception, so ingenious in its varied arrangement of figures, and so powerful that in comparison, according to some, all other paintings there look like playing cards."

Rembrandt's pupil Samuel van Hoogstraten
on *The Company of Captain Frans Banning Cocq,*
also known as *The Night Watch*

CHAPTER III
LONELINESS AND BANKRUPTCY

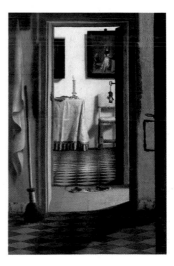

In *The Night Watch* (detail opposite) the eyes peering out beyond the blade of a sword, slightly knowing, are Rembrandt's. A very different tone is set by *The Slippers* (right), painted by Samuel van Hoogstraten.

Nobody doubted Rembrandt's genius. Indeed it was because nobody doubted it that people criticized. The way in which they did so, unfortunately, given that he depended entirely on commissions, proved highly damaging. He was accused of painting "too much to please himself": An artist was expected, rather, to meet the requirements of those who commissioned his work. Rembrandt might have produced a work of art, but what he had been engaged to do was paint a group portrait—no more, no less. This amounted to false pretenses.

The Genius That Dazzled Art Lovers and Collectors Did Not Stop Clients from Quibbling

It was not genius that clients paid for but an identifiable image: A portrait should be a likeness. Rembrandt, on the other hand, was painting an inner self, an elusive essence, a metamorphosis. Some of Rembrandt's pupils began to find more acceptance with the public than their master did. Rembrandt's driving desire was simply to paint, to test the limits of his art.

A few months after Saskia's death he painted a portrait of her to pair with a self-portrait signed and dated "Rembrandt f 1643." In this picture he is defying death: Painted, he and Saskia stand together, eternalized as art. For him, a portrait like this was akin to painting the mysteries of the Old and New Testaments: The same subjects, death and resurrection, were given expression by his brush. In Rembrandt's mind *seeing* was indeed *believing*.

Genius Won Him Respect and Admiration— but Acceptance?

Whether or not he was accepted did not concern Rembrandt. He continued to paint and etch.

Rembrandt engaged a nurse to look after Titus. She was a stalwart countrywoman from the north called Geertje Dircx, the widow of Abraham Claeszoon, a trumpeter.

This left Rembrandt free to concentrate on his art. He found subjects everywhere: the slanting rays across a lightly clouded sky in this landscape,

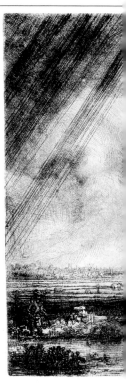

Geertje Dircx, Titus' nurse, drawn by Rembrandt c. 1642.

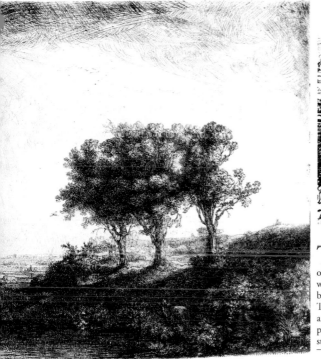

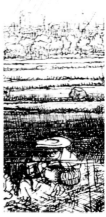

The storm passes over the summer sky of *The Three Trees* (left, with detail above), etched by Rembrandt in 1643. The opposition of light and shade, startling in its precision, conveys both stillness and energy.

The Three Trees, a pig lying down, a scholar lost in thought, a monk taking a tumble with a girl in the corn, subjects from the Old and New Testaments, beggars, and naked men. He did not tailor his inspiration to the norms of Calvinist good taste. His models dreamed, prayed, or sinned as he himself painted, prayed, and sinned.

He took his young son's nurse as his mistress.

The words attributed to Rembrandt by Arnold Houbraken have the ring of truth: "When I wish to occupy my mind, I do not care so much for honor as I do for liberty." But Rembrandt had more to do than

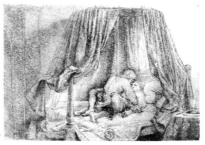

It was not Rembrandt who named this etching *Le Lit à la Française*, a title not entirely reflecting the print's subject.

pass judgment on his own life. He lived for and through his painting. Everything was subordinate to his art and dedicated to it.

By the End of the 1640s Rembrandt Was Painting Fewer Commissioned Portraits

Old men daydreaming, bedecked in chains, caps upon their heads and young girls in reverie, elbows propped on a windowsill, or hands upon a door were subjects that did not need to be commissioned. Nor did paintings of stories from the Bible. Thus Rembrandt painted *The Woman Taken in Adultery, The Holy Family with the Curtain, The Adoration of the Shepherds, Joseph's Dream,* and *Anna Accused by Tobit of Stealing the Kid. The Woman Taken in Adultery* and *Circumcision* were bought by the stadtholder for 2400 guilders in November 1646. In shape and size they were very like the pictures he had bought seven years earlier. Whereas the stadtholder had previously commissioned paintings, he was now buying finished works. This signified a change in Rembrandt's relationship with his clients.

Unconfirmed Anecdotes and Comments Were Recorded Long After Rembrandt's Death

The first is recounted by Filippo Baldinucci: "After it had become commonly known that whoever wanted to be portrayed by him had to sit to him for some two or three months, there were few who came forward. The cause of his slowness was that, immediately after the first work had dried, he took it up again.... When he worked he would not have granted an audience to the first monarch in the world, who would have had to return and return again until he had found him no longer engaged upon that work."

The second is related by Arnold Houbraken: "[Rembrandt] often drew ten versions of a face before

Is the figure in *St. Jerome Beside a Pollard Willow* (below) engaged in translating the Bible? Rembrandt etched this appealing image of the hermit's life in 1648.

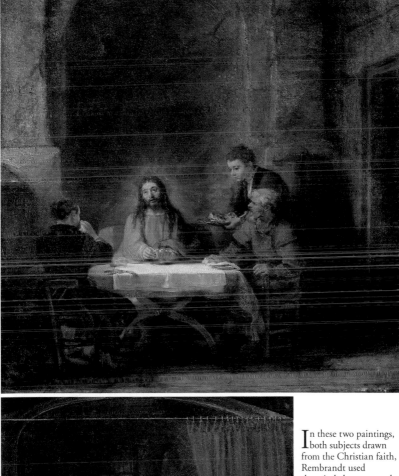

In these two paintings, both subjects drawn from the Christian faith, Rembrandt used theatrical elements rarely found in his work. In *Christ at Emmaus* (above) a stone alcove is the backdrop to the figure of Christ, while the open drapery in *The Holy Family with the Curtain* (left) frames the scene like a stage set.

reproducing one on the canvas; he could spend an entire day, even two, determining the arrangement of a turban in the way that most pleased him."

The last also comes from Houbraken: "One day he was working on a large group portrait featuring a couple and their children. He had nearly finished it when his monkey died. Not having another canvas at hand, he included the dead monkey in the work in progress. Naturally his models could scarcely tolerate the unappetizing relic featured at their side; but the effect produced by the corpse so impressed the artist that rather than remove it to satisfy his clients he left the work unfinished."

Rembrandt's Demands Became Intolerable to the Clients He Was Supposed to Satisfy: They Began to Abandon Him

As they forsook him, Rembrandt learned to make do without his clients. His life began to be characterized by extravagance, even scandal. He was constantly buying—in salesrooms, from dealers, peddlers, or sellers of old clothes.

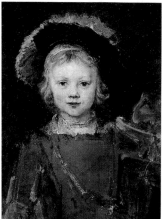

"He began to buy old clothes that struck him as strange and picturesque; and even when they were utterly filthy he hung them on the wall in his workshop, alongside the beautiful curiosities he had taken pleasure in collecting, such as ancient and modern weapons of all kinds—arrows, halberds, daggers, swords, knives—an inordinate quantity of prints, medals, and exquisite drawings, and many other objects he thought might be of use to a painter. At the same time he deserves much praise for a particular generosity, however extravagant it might have been in reality. He held his craft in such high esteem that when anything connected with it was offered at auction, such as paintings and drawings by great artists in various fields, he would offer such a high sum that nobody could outbid him; he said that he did this to build up the prestige of his profession."

There seems no reason to doubt this and other hearsay reports Baldinucci recounted. Saskia had left Rembrandt

This portrait is thought to be of Rembrandt's son, Titus, born in 1641, which would suggest a date of about 1650 for the picture.

approximately 40,000 guilders. That he should have spent a part of it buying old materials and objects supposedly needed for his painting—or for the prestige of his profession—was regarded, at best, as irresponsible. The Amsterdam of money markets, banks, and businesses did not approve of extravagance.

Calvinist Amsterdam Looked Askance at Any Hint of Debauchery

The young Hendrickje Stoffelsdochter Jaegher (usually known as Hendrickje Stoffels) had been living in the house in Sint Anthoniesdijk for some time before she became Rembrandt's mistress in 1649. This development was not welcomed by Geertje Dircx, who had filled the role for years. On 24 January 1648 Geertje had dictated a will appointing Titus her heir. All her assets, including Saskia's jewelry, which Rembrandt had given her, were left to him.

This drawing (c. 1642) of a woman in the peasant dress of northern Holland is thought to be a portrait of Geertje Dircx, Titus' nurse and Rembrandt's mistress. She caused many problems for the artist, and he seems not to have painted her very often.

This will was put forward as evidence a few months later when she brought a case of breach of promise against Rembrandt. The tribunal dismissed her action but set a figure of 200 guilders per year to be paid by Rembrandt to Geertje Dircx in compensation for rescinding the revocation of her will. (Rembrandt had offered 166 guilders.)

Some time afterward he tried to recover Saskia's jewelry. Crippled with debt, Geertje had pawned all the pieces. Rembrandt took her before the court and accused her of a dissolute life. On 23 October 1649 she was condemned to twelve years of solitary confinement with hard labor. Rembrandt was made responsible for the cost of transporting her to Gouda (in southwestern

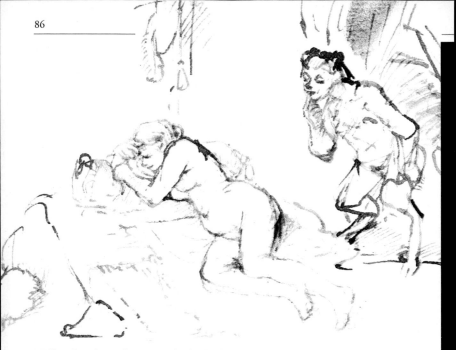

Holland), where she was to be locked away, and he had to continue paying her allowance.

Rembrandt Besieged by Jealous Spirits

Hendrickje Stoffels had been a witness in the case. She was twenty-four years old, possibly only twenty-three. Rembrandt was twenty years older. He made no attempt to hide the fact that she lived with him as his wife. Like everyone in his entourage, she posed for him. But he did not marry her, as this would have meant renouncing his life interest in the inheritance left to him by Saskia.

Rembrandt went on spending. He began to fall into debt. The former owners of the house in Sint Anthoniesdijk had still not been paid in full.

His reputation as an artist, however, remained untarnished by court proceedings and his financial situation. Lambert van den Bos wrote a poem in 1650 acclaiming the collection of Marten Kretzer, which included works by Titian and Rubens: "I shall not drive

The Sleeping Nymph and a Satyr in the drawing above are an allusion to Titian's *Jupiter and Antiope*.

There is the hint of a smile on the face of this elegant woman. A muted brilliance lights only her face, the pearls in her jewelry, and her bosom. The look in her eyes betrays intimacy with the artist. The portrait is generally thought to be of Hendrickje Stoffels. She posed for Rembrandt as had Saskia, whose place and role she had assumed.

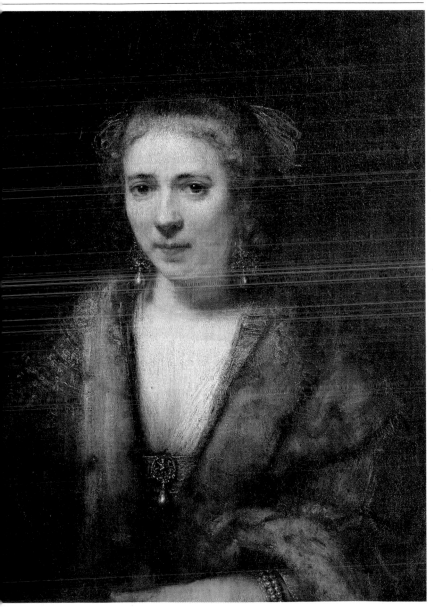

myself to prove your renown, O Rembrandt, with the scratches of my pen, as the esteem in which you are held everywhere emerges with the sole mention of your name."

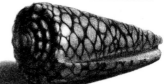

Nonetheless there was no escaping the two experts who came during 1650 to make an inventory of Rembrandt's Sint Anthoniesdijk house. His collections were valued at 17,000 guilders. Of the total, Rembrandt's own paintings accounted for 6400 guilders. His capital worth perhaps reassured his creditors. For the moment they took no further action.

Merchants and Politicians Forsook His Studio. People of a More Intellectual Bent Were Drawn There Instead

With the passage of years those most often to be found in Rembrandt's company seemed to be given to writing, study, commentary, painting—creativity. Jan Cornelisz Sylvius was a theologian and preacher. Hendrick

In the year 1650 Rembrandt concentrated on etching landscapes, with the exception of *The Shell* (above). The image perhaps symbolized the riches brought by foreign trade; however, it seems more likely that Rembrandt was fascinated by the perfect structure of its spirals and the patterned smoothness of its surface.

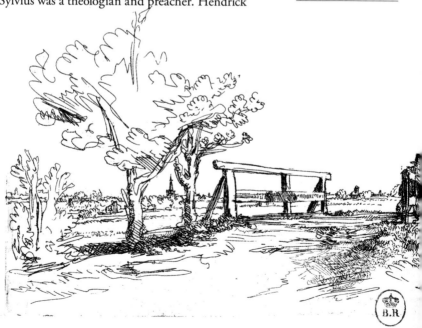

Martensz Sorgh was a painter. Dr. Ephraim Bueno was one of the foremost doctors and writers in Amsterdam. Rembrandt etched or painted their portraits.

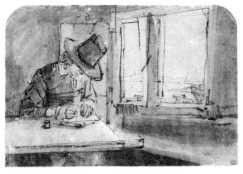

Another companion, Jan Six, aspired to more than the status of burgomaster of Amsterdam. He wrote poetry and tragedies. In 1648, the year after Rembrandt etched the first portrait of him, standing with his back to the window reading, he published a long tragedy in verse, *Medea*. He belonged to a noble family that had fled St. Omer (northern France). He had studied at the University of Leiden and made a tour of Italy in 1640. In 1652 he gave up business. Sometimes he invited Rembrandt to stay on an estate he owned on the Diemerdyke. There Rembrandt drew landscapes and

Jan Six at His Desk, a drawing by Rembrandt dated 1655. In 1652 Jan Six had retired from business to devote himself to writing. He is also featured in Rembrandt's etching *Six' Bridge* (below left), dated 1645.

completed two drawings for the *Album Amicorum* by Six.

Like Rembrandt, Jan Six collected antiques, enamels, and other objets d'art. But the means at his disposal were different.

Rembrandt's Creditors Grew Uneasy

Might they have been placated by the news that a nobleman from Messina, Don Antonio Ruffo, had commissioned a work from him—"a philosopher," without further specification? It seems unlikely. Rembrandt talked painting. His creditors talked money. That he painted was of no interest to them: They wanted him to pay.

By 1653 some of his creditors could wait no longer. The United Provinces had suffered setbacks in a war against England, and crisis ensued. The stock exchange was in trouble. Rembrandt had to borrow money. Jan Six loaned him 1000 guilders. Lodewijk van Ludick was guarantor. Cornelis Witsen, former burgomaster of Amsterdam, and the merchant Isaac van Heertsbeeck each loaned 4000 guilders. All Rembrandt's assets, possibly including his paintings, were offered as security for these loans. The *Portrait of Saskia in a Red Hat* and *St. John the Baptist Preaching* joined Jan Six' collection. Rembrandt had never managed to finish paying for his house in Sint Anthoniesdijk; in February 1653 Christoffel Thijsz, the previous owner, presented an account showing that 8470 guilders, interest included, was still outstanding.

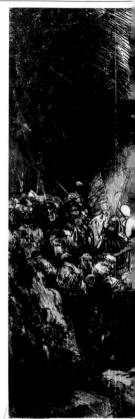

Rembrandt and Hendrickje in Court

Hendrickje and Rembrandt were summoned to appear before the ecclesiastical court. There

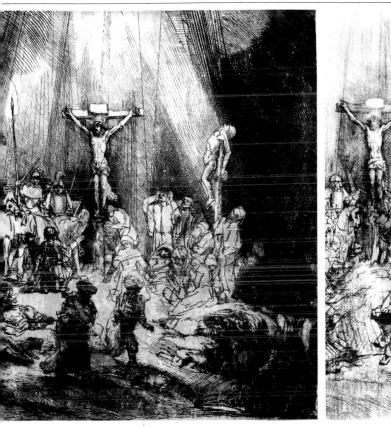

they were to answer accusations of living together unmarried. They refused. In July 1654 the consistory of the Calvinist church cited Hendrickje again, and she alone. Why was Rembrandt not accused? We have no answer. Hendrickje received many more summonses, which she ignored. When at last she appeared before the judges, she was exhorted to renounce her illicit relationship and do penance. She continued to live with Rembrandt.

In October 1654, in the Oudekerk, the church where Saskia had been laid to rest, a daughter of Rembrandt and Hendrickje was baptized and named Cornelia.

Both in its size (15.5 x 18 inches) and in its dramatic use of the effects of light and shade, *The Three Crosses* (1653) ranks as one of Rembrandt's most important etchings. Above are the first state (left) and a detail from the fourth state (right). Opposite: *The Woman Taken in Adultery.*

In 1654 Rembrandt Again Failed to Meet His Debts

Once again he had to negotiate an agreement with
Thijsz. He pledged a yearly payment of 50 guilders.
Thijsz could hardly have been under any illusion. He
knew that Rembrandt had few commissions, and he
knew the sums he was paid for them.

Cornelis Eysbert van Goor, who had represented
the Sicilian noble Antonio Ruffo, sent Rembrandt
500 guilders for *Aristotle Contemplating the Bust of
Homer*, the "philosopher" commissioned in 1652.

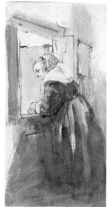

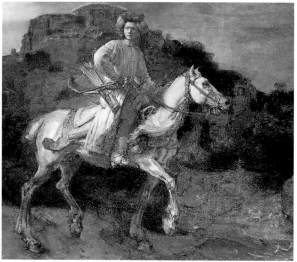

Lacking the legal
status of wife to
Rembrandt, Hendrickje
—in name, at least—was
never officially linked to
his pictures. Her face and
figure nonetheless
featured in a good many
of them, which were
given titles such as
*Woman Looking Out of the
Window* (above).

The canvas is signed and dated 1653. Months of work
had been involved.

As for other work, Thijsz must have been aware that
Rembrandt refused to comply with some of his clients'
requirements. For example, Diego Andrada, a merchant,
commissioned a portrait of a girl, for which he paid a
deposit of 65 guilders. The rest was to be paid on
delivery of the painting. Andrada did not find that there
was any likeness and asked to be reimbursed. Intolerant
of criticism, Rembrandt replied by demanding the
rest of his fee. Clients were not willing to accept this sort
of intransigence.

For centuries *The Polish
Rider* (above left)
was accepted as the
work of Rembrandt. In
recent years, however,
doubts have been cast
on its authenticity by
some experts. Another
"Rembrandt" to be
removed from the
catalogue of the artist's
works is *The Man with
the Golden Helmet*.

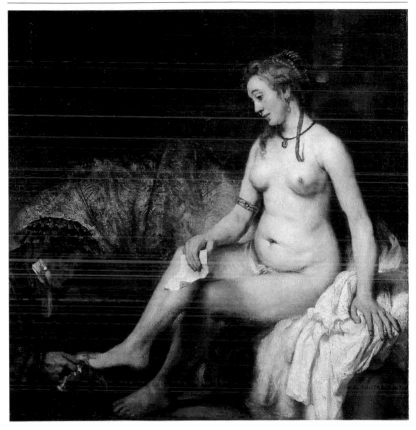

By May 1656 Rembrandt Was in Desperate Straits

On 17 May he applied to the Court of Orphans to transfer the title of the house in Sint Anthoniesdijk to Titus. He agreed to remain responsible for all debts. The court refused. One of Rembrandt's brothers in Leiden was declared a pauper, and his sister was close to insolvency.

The court appointed a guardian to determine the respective shares of Titus and his father.

On 20 July 1656 the High Court appointed Frans Janszoon Bruningh to liquidate Rembrandt's assets.

Rembrandt painted *Bathsheba* in 1654. Bathsheba, suffering David's cruelty, and Hendrickje, hounded by the Church, were linked by a spirit of forced resignation.

Overleaf, left: *A Woman Bathing in a Stream*, 1655. Overleaf, right: *Hendrickje (?) at the Window*, 1656–7.

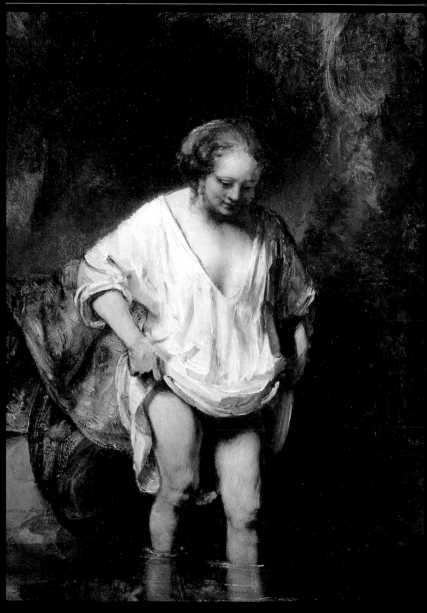

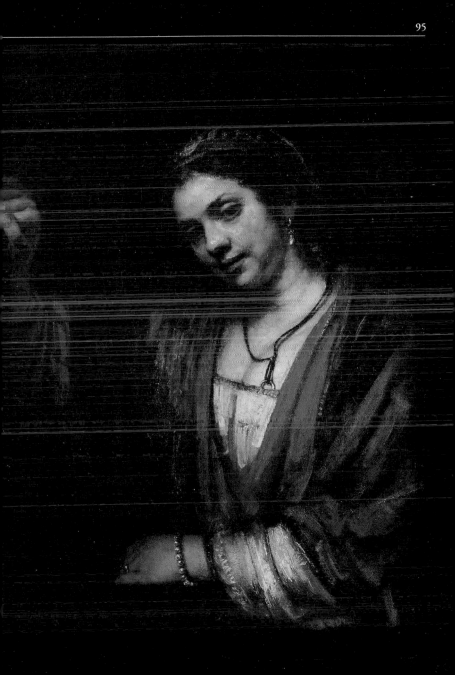

The painter had successfully petitioned the court to apply the principle of a *cessio bonorum*. This was generally done only for debtors of acknowledged good faith. The pretext of damages and losses suffered at sea was accepted by the court, sparing Rembrandt the disgrace of bankruptcy and a prison sentence.

On 25 and 26 July 1656 an Inventory of the Entire Contents of the House on Sint Anthoniesbreestraat Was Prepared

The list included 363 items (see pp. 130–5). Everything was scrupulously written down: the linen at the laundry, nos. 359–63; "a pewter water jug," no. 351; "a sculpture of the Emperor Augustus," no. 147; "2 pillows," no. 133; "an East Indian sewing box," no. 150; "47 specimens of land and sea animals and the like," no. 175; "a portrait head by Raphael of Urbino," no. 67;

Dangling a pencil case in front of his desk, Titus seems to be lost in thought, perhaps about his next drawing (below left). The inventory of Rembrandt's possessions mentioned "three little dogs done from life by Titus van Rijn." Also listed was a book of drawings by Titian, including two studies for *The Death of St. Peter Martyr* (opposite). Below is a drawing by Rembrandt of the parable of *The Unjust Steward.*

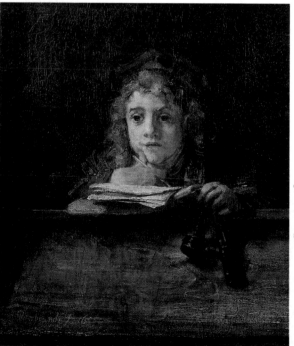

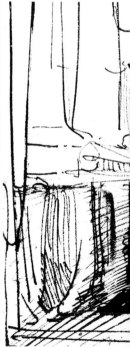

"1 book filled with drawings of all Roman buildings and views by all the most excellent masters," no. 240; "a small metal cannon," no. 335; "a *Raising of Lazarus* by Jan Lievensz," no. 42, and so on.

A fabulous collection of paintings by Adriaen Brouwer, Jan Lievens, Hercules Seghers, Palma Vecchio, Pieter Lastman, Govaert Jansz Flinck, Jan Porcellis, Lucas van Valckenburgh, Jacopo Bassano, Raphael, Jan van Eyck, Giorgione... A fabulous collection of dozens of portfolios full of engravings by Pieter Brueghel the Elder, Lucas Cranach the Elder, Antonio Tempesta, Lucas van Leyden, Rubens, Jacob Jordaens, Jacques Callo... A fabulous collection of engraved reproductions of works by Titian, Raphael, Michelangelo, Annibale Carracci, Giovanni Battista Rosso ("Fiorentino"), and Giulio Bonasone... The house in which Rembrandt painted was packed with masterpieces.

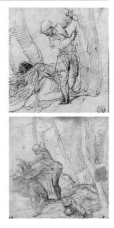

On the Point of Being Stripped of All His Possessions, Rembrandt Painted a Second Anatomy Lesson

Professor Tholinx was a relative of both Jan Six and Professor Tulp. It was doubtless at Tulp's suggestion that Dr. Johannes Deyman, who succeeded him as inspector of the medical colleges in Amsterdam, commissioned another anatomy lesson from Rembrandt. The lessons were now held in the lecture room where *The Anatomy Lesson of Professor Tulp* had been hung. Deyman's portrait was to be displayed in the same room.

The first anatomy lesson had brought Rembrandt fame and fortune in Amsterdam. Twenty-four years later he had to prove that, in spite of adversity, he remained the greatest painter in Holland.

The Anatomy Lesson: **Facing an Old Challenge the Second Time**

Originally, on either side of the prone corpse, there were painted eight men. At Dr. Deyman's side his assistant held the top of the skull. Sir Joshua Reynolds, who saw the canvas before a fire in 1723 destroyed three-quarters of it, observed that the colors resembled those of Titian.

Titian is not the only artist of the Italian Renaissance evoked by the painting. The way the corpse is laid out recalls Mantegna's *Dead Christ.* The inventory of Rembrandt's house mentions, as item no. 200, "the precious book of Andrea Mantegna."

The Auction of Rembrandt's Possessions Started in September 1656

The curiosities were sold. The paintings went under the gavel in December 1657. Disputes between the creditors then stopped further sales for some months. In February 1658 the house in Sint Anthoniesdijk was sold for 11,218 guilders. This sum, by no means negligible in a recession, did not, however, cover Rembrandt's debts.

In September 1658 the collection of prints and drawings was sold, despite attempts to preserve it. The sale was advertised: "The administrator of the property of the painter Rembrandt van Rijn has been authorized

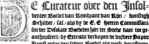

This notice advertised the sale of Rembrandt's collection of prints and drawings at the Keizerskroon Inn in September 1658.

A fire in 1723 destroyed three-quarters of *The Anatomy Lesson of Dr. Johannes Deyman* (opposite). Of Deyman, only the hands remain visible and, of the eight spectators originally positioned in symmetrical fashion around the surgeon, only his assistant survives, holding the top of the corpse's skull in his left hand. More accurately informed than in 1632, Rembrandt this time featured the dissected abdomen.

by their Honors, the Commissioners of the Chamber of Insolvent Estates, to sell by executive order the works of art in said estate, consisting of works by various prominent Italian, French, German, and Netherlandish masters, which the said Rembrandt van Rijn has assembled by his care. At the same time, a large number of drawings and sketches by the said Rembrandt van Rijn himself will be offered for sale. The sale will take place on the day, hour, and year stated above, at the house of Barent Jansz Schuurman, innkeeper of the Keizerskroon [The Emperor's Crown], on the Calverstraat, where the previous sale was held."

The sale took place, and everything was dispersed—for the paltry sum of 600 guilders.

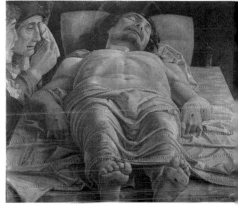

Rembrandt owned an engraving of Mantegna's *Dead Christ,* 1506 (above), which was the model for *The Anatomy Lesson of Dr. Johannes Deyman* (below).

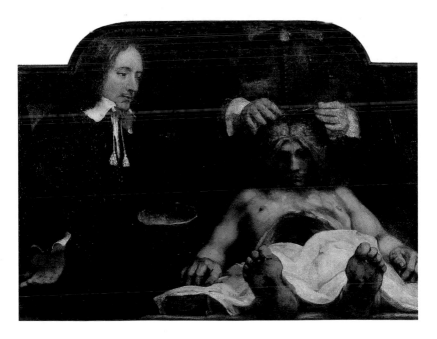

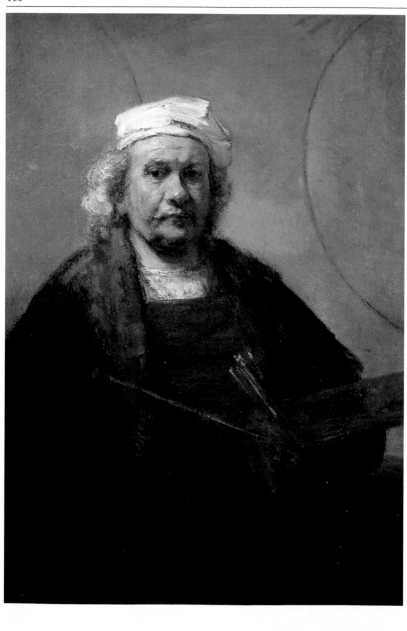

In the denuded house in Sint Anthoniesdijk that no longer belonged to him Rembrandt read the verses by H. F. Waterloos extolling his portrait of the poet Jeremias de Decker. Did his bankruptcy, poor reputation, and alienation worry him? Ruined and rejected, he still knew his own worth.

CHAPTER IV
RETIREMENT AND DEATH

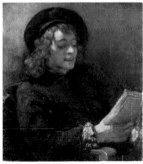

This *Self-Portrait* (detail opposite) of Rembrandt in a heavy coat with a wide brown collar, a white cap upon the tangle of his grizzled locks, was painted c. 1663. The circles in the background represent time. This portrait of the artist's son, *Titus Reading* (left), was done a few years earlier.

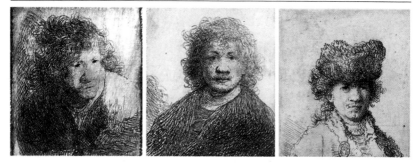

In the very year that he was stripped in the auction rooms of all that had once represented his ambition (1658), he painted a self-portrait: Seated, grave, serene, he holds a cane in the fingers of his left hand. It is a portrait of self-assurance and power, a portrait of Rembrandt's pride. At the end of the day it mattered little to him that nothing was left. He could still paint.

Rembrandt in the Mirror of Art

It would not be his last self-portrait. He painted, drew, or etched his own portrait approximately one hundred times. No other artist has matched him in this. He featured himself in 1625 in the crowd stoning St. Stephen, in 1626 with a harp in his hands (in *A Musical Gathering*), in 1665 bursting with laughter as Zeuxis, the painter of antiquity. He showed himself in all moods: apprehensive, mirthful, debonair, confident, conceited, arrogant, and disillusioned. He painted the onset of the years—puffy features, wrinkles, the ravages of age. It mattered little to him: His portraits did not aim for likeness. In rags or in finery, it was isolation that he studied; an isolation that he tried, perhaps despairingly, to counter with an assurance that proved elusive.

Rembrandt's self-portraits were not a narrative of his life, but the incarnation of his ambitions as a painter. His portraits were studies in which he used his own face to explore a range of expressions or attitudes, as if drawing up a catalogue. His portraits are declarations. Creating his own version of a Titian or Raphael, he

No model was ever more readily or more freely available to Rembrandt than Rembrandt himself. He executed an abundance of self-portraits. This was not only a way of studying the range of expression on a face and exploring different artistic techniques; it was also a form of quest for affirmation, a plea, a cry, a record of a lifetime's changing attitudes and emotions. Perhaps he did a hundred or so, but it is difficult to be precise about the number of Rembrandt's self-portraits. Some may well have been copies by his pupils, or copies which he himself revised, or contemporary fakes, or different versions of the same portrait done by his own hand. All of this makes a definitive catalogue an impossibility.

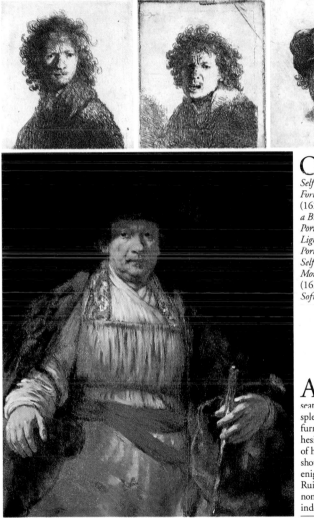

Opposite and above, from left to right: *Self-Portrait, Leaning Forward, as if Listening* (1628); *Self-Portrait with a Broad Nose* (1628); *Self-Portrait in Fur Cap and Light Dress* (1630); *Self-Portrait Angry* (1630); *Self-Portrait Open-Mouthed, as if Shouting* (1630); *Self-Portrait in a Soft Cap* (1634).

A 1658 self-portrait shows Rembrandt seated in solitary splendor, confident, with furrowed brow, a smile hesitating at the corners of his mouth (left). How should one interpret his enigmatic trappings? Ruined, Rembrandt was nonetheless declaring his indestructible strength.

proved he knew the great masters, the landmarks in the history of art. His portraits are prayers. He painted himself as a sinner helping to raise the cross upon which Christ was laid, and as a prodigal son.

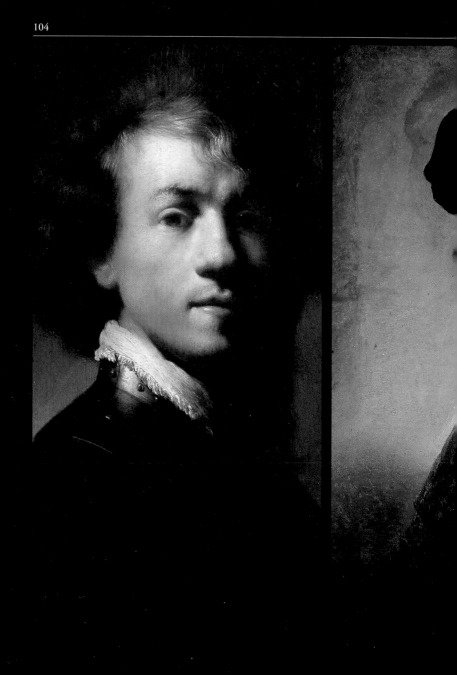

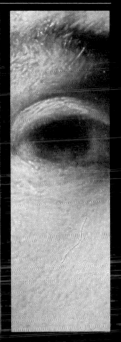

Rembrandt Upright, Confident, Unconquered

In these two self-portraits—dated 1629 (opposite and detail above) and 1634 (left)—Rembrandt is wearing the same piece of armor: a steel neck-piece that he used to identify himself with the soldier citizens of the United Provinces, who had just won freedom for their country. He had not served in any militia, but he demonstrated a form of patriotism that he shared with many of his clients.

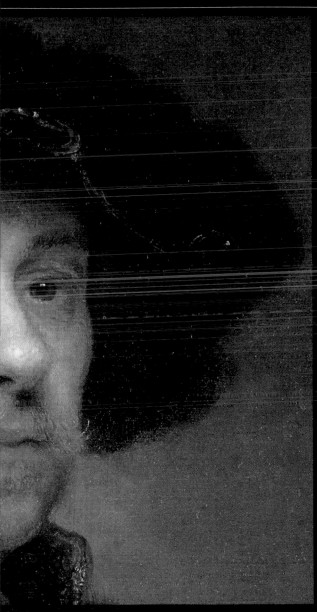

The Master

Wearing the familiar broad cap, decked with gold, furs, velvet, and embroidery, Rembrandt rests his arm on a narrow parapet in this *Self Portrait* of 1640. His pose is that of Baldassare Castiglione in the portrait by Raphael, which Rembrandt had copied at the auction where the dealer Alphonso Lopez acquired the work. The richness of the Venetian colors also evokes another picture in Lopez' possession: the painting by Titian of a man in blue sleeves, often entitled *Portrait of Ariosto*. Rembrandt thus appropriated and assimilated the "inventions" of the Italian artists for this portrait painted in Amsterdam. A sojourn in Italy was not indispensable.

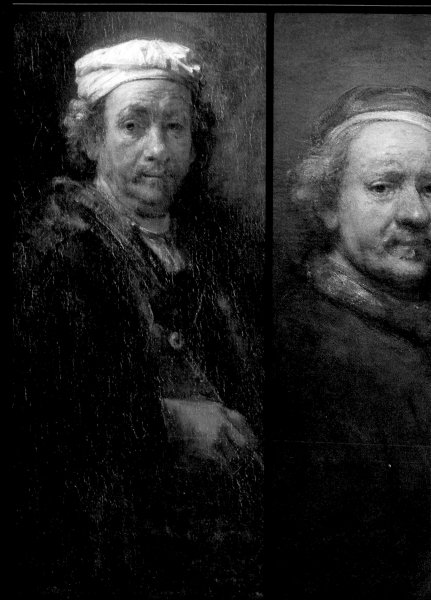

The Last Years

In these three self-portraits (details left) from the 1660s, there are no extraneous trappings, no pomp: The hair has gone gray; the face has become wrinkled and plump; a look in the eye speaks of weariness and regret, but remains impassive. Rembrandt added gold lines to the white cap, bringing it into harmony with the background, the hair, and the face, as if the painter were merging into his painting.

He painted to save his soul and his reputation. His portraits are portraits of a quest, of his isolation. He was powerless and alone, except for his art.

Money Was a Continual Problem for Rembrandt

In 1658 Rembrandt still owed the 1000 guilders Jan Six had loaned him in 1653. The debt had passed into the hands of a merchant and collector, Lodewijk van Ludick, who required the money, interest and capital, to be repaid in three years, plus a painting as a form of supplementary dividend. Rembrandt did not meet either of these conditions.

Rembrandt was no longer concerned with the legal issues outstanding but with Titus' portion of his inheritance. Some of the creditors, considering themselves ill treated, were claiming that the 1647 valuation had overestimated Titus' share.

Witnesses were called to prove it valid. The judges took evidence from two men who had each paid 100 guilders for their portraits in *The Company of Captain Frans Banning Cocq*, from van Ludick—who had bought a Rubens from Rembrandt—from the artist Philips Koninck, and from the silversmith Jan van Loo and his wife, who gave a description of Saskia's jewelry. The judges were favorably convinced by the evidence.

On 18 December 1660 Rembrandt Finally Left the House on Sint Anthoniesbreestraat: All Was Sold, All Debts Settled

He spent several days in the Keizerskroon Inn, the very place where his collections of drawings and etchings had been sold in 1657 and 1658. Then he moved into a narrow house on the Rozengracht in the Jordaan district, inhabited by artisans and shopkeepers. It lay to the west,

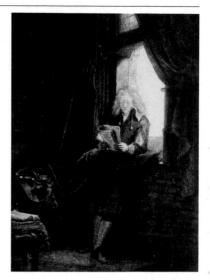

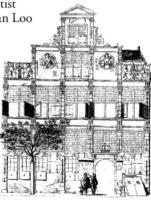

Jan Six (above), whom Rembrandt etched in 1647, had often saved him from bankruptcy. Rembrandt's worldly goods were sold in the Keizerskroon Inn (below).

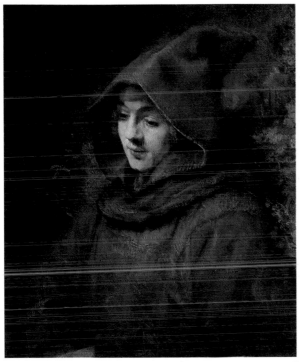

Rembrandt took his son as the model for this portrait, *Titus in Friar's Habit,* of 1660. Did he portray Titus in this way for the pleasure of exploring every shade of brown on the sackcloth robe? Did he wish to direct the gaze of the viewer to the paleness of the face? Or did he simply think Titus a suitable model for St. Francis of Assisi?

beyond the Keizersgracht, the outermost of the three canals around the center of the city. In this house, rented for 225 guilders a year, he returned to his painting.

On 15 December he had countersigned an agreement, drawn up by a notary, that made Titus and Hendrickje responsible for him. The rules of the Guild of St. Luke, the association of painters that Rembrandt had joined in 1634, left him no alternative: His bankruptcy barred him from trading in the city. Titus and Hendrickje undertook to feed, lodge, and help Rembrandt, who in turn had to acknowledge them as his creditors. He owed 800 guilders to one, 950 guilders to the other. All his work—canvases, drawings, etchings—was to be theirs until his death. And it was to remain at their disposal for six years afterward.

The occasional pupil still came to Rembrandt, one

being Aert de Gelder, and the occasional portrait was
commissioned. He was unconcerned, painting Jacob
Jacobsz Trip as he would have painted an apostle.

The faces he painted at this period, whether of Christ,
saints, rabbis, men, or women, evoke solitude and a calm
gravity, a state of mind akin to Rembrandt's own. His
work was giving expression to legends and visions,
haunted by images from the Bible.

The City of Amsterdam Commissioned Him to Paint a Vision of a Different Kind: The National Pride of Holland

The commission had first been given to Govaert Flinck,
Rembrandt's former pupil, who died having done only
a rough sketch. The painting, *The Conspiracy of Julius
Civilis*, was supposed to demonstrate the strength of
Holland's will for independence, proved in the revolts
against Rome and Spain. The Dutch compared
their recent struggles to the revolt of the Batavians
against the Romans, as recounted by Tacitus. It was
at a banquet given by their leader Julius Civilis that
the Batavians had sworn to put an end to Roman
occupation. The finished work was to hang in the
town hall.

In 1662 Rembrandt's Painting Was Completed and Placed in Position

It hung there for only a few months before it was taken
down. *The Conspiracy of Julius Civilis* was returned to
Rembrandt. Another painting was then commissioned
from Joris Ovens, who reverted to Flinck's sketch,
representing Civilis in profile.

What did the elect of Amsterdam dislike in
Rembrandt's work? Was it the way the light falling on
the array of arms held out over the table exposed Civilis'
destroyed eye? Legends should not feature the one-eyed
—a symbol should be without blemish; pride knew no
handicap. Perhaps there were objections to the way the
paint was applied: The rough marks of the palette knife
did not accord with the desired note of ostentation.

Rembrandt was left to cut down the canvas of some
twenty square feet to more salable proportions.

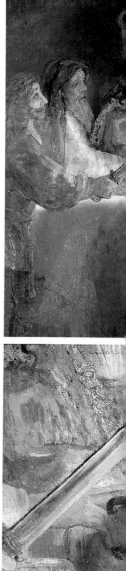

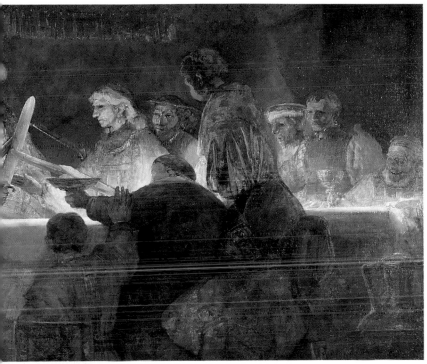

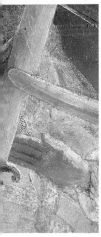

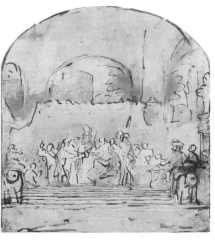

Rediscovered in 1891 in a Stockholm museum under another title, *The Conspiracy of Julius Civilis* (above and detail far left) represents only a quarter of the original composition. Was this the result of fire or a deliberate attempt to diminish the power and realism of the scene? An impression of the scale of the original work can be seen in the preparatory drawing (left).

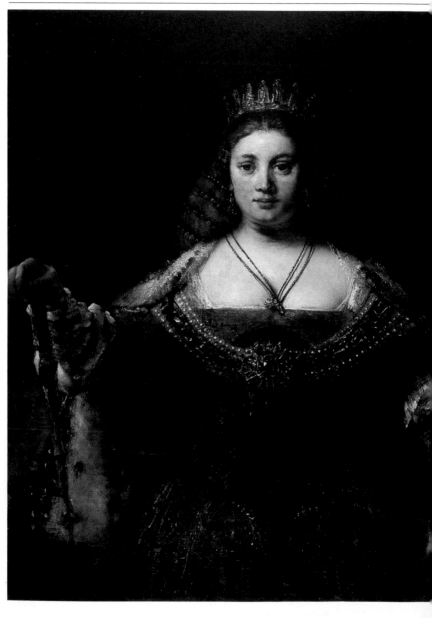

Rembrandt's Manner of Painting Upset His Clients and Even Troubled Art Lovers

Some years after Rembrandt's death, in *Discourse on the Lives and Works of the Most Excellent Ancient and Modern Painters*, published in 1685, the French writer André Félibien wrote: "All his works are painted in a very individual manner, very different from that ordinarily used by Flemish painters, which seems so overrefined. For he often uses large brushstrokes and applies thick layers of color, one after the other, without blending and softening them. Nevertheless, as tastes vary, a number of people have formed a high opinion of his work."

Early in the 18th century Arnold Houbraken observed: "He always handled his paintings in the same manner: I have seen several in which some details are executed with the greatest of care, while the rest seem to be painted with a house painter's brush, without the slightest heed paid to the design. However, he could not stop himself working like this, and he justified himself by saying that he considered a picture finished when the master had achieved his intentions." This account rings true. There is in any case little doubt that it was not around the wishes of his clients that Rembrandt shaped his work.

Houbraken again: "It is said that one day he was painting a portrait so loaded with color that one could have lifted the picture by seizing the figure by the nose. One sees in his canvases precious stones and pearl necklaces or turbans executed with so much impasto that they seem to be in relief; and it is because of this manner of painting that his pictures make such a great impression when viewed at a distance."

A New Commission

Cut down, the canvas of *The Conspiracy of Julius Civilis* was little larger than the portrait of a guild meeting commissioned from Rembrandt by the clothmakers of Amsterdam. *The Portrait of the Syndics of the Clothmakers' Guild* was to hang in the guild headquarters. It shows five men in black hats grouped

The imposing and regal portrait of *Juno* (opposite and detail below) was no doubt painted by Rembrandt to mollify the impatient collector Harmen Becker. While the face, the necklace, and the right hand communicate power, the details are neglected, and the left hand and arm are barely sketched in.

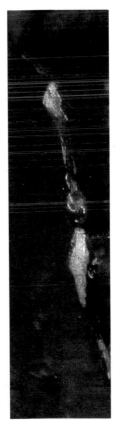

around a table covered with a carpet (with a secretary in the background). The focus of attention is an open book, one man's hand poised to turn the page. Perhaps they are checking accounts? Rembrandt has caught them at a moment when they have been interrupted. They raise their eyes and turn their heads. Someone enters. The syndics look at him—or at us, looking at the painting. They dominate. Their imperceptibly lowered gaze and the perspective from which the table is presented imply that the picture is at a good height; viewers have to raise their eyes to look at the men who are gathered there.

It is not certain whether the group consists of Jan Bitter, Cornelis Egbertsz Cover, Willem van Renevelt, Servaes del Court, and Jan Jansz Arentburg—who in the years 1661 and 1662 were in charge of cloth control —or of Willem van Doyenburg, Volkert Janszoon, Jacob van Loon, Aernout van der Mye, and Joachem de Neve—responsible in the same period for checking samples. Nor does it matter.

Quite apart from being a portrait of individuals, the work is a portrait of authority and power. The magistrates of Amsterdam rejected Rembrandt's *The Conspiracy of Julius Civilis* because it did not conform to the myth in their minds. *The Syndics*, painted the following year, 1662, was different: As the magistrates raised their eyes to the painting they were forced to recognize the power it conveyed.

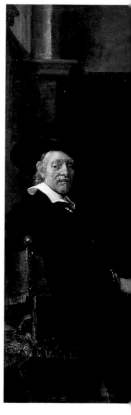

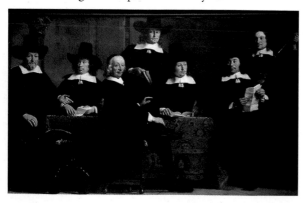

A last group painting, *The Portrait of the Syndics of the Cloth-makers' Guild* (above), was commissioned by Amsterdam's cloth-makers' guild, which still accepted Rembrandt's genius. *The Guild of Wine Merchants* (left) is by Rembrandt's pupil Ferdinand Bol. The drawing (right) is a study for *The Syndics*.

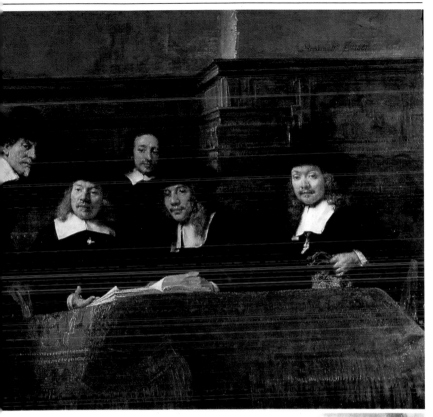

Did the Aging Painter Still Seek Recognition by the Bourgeoisie?

In a poem published in 1662 Jan Vos acclaimed Rembrandt as one of the most celebrated painters in Amsterdam. He was recognized as a master in all of Europe.

Rembrandt knew that his works were in the most important European collections—including those of the king of England and Cardinal Richelieu. He had in 1661 sent a second painting, *Alexander the Great,* to Don Antonio Ruffo in Messina, Sicily, for which he was paid 500 guilders.

Having in 1660 received a letter from Italian painter Guercino, in which he described Rembrandt as a virtuoso on the strength of a few prints he had seen, Ruffo commissioned another painting from him, on Homer.

Was it because Ruffo's commissions accorded well with his own ideas (he had painted *Aristotle Contemplating the Bust of Homer* for Ruffo in 1653) that Rembrandt was willing to heed his criticisms? When Ruffo objected to the way four pieces of canvas had been sewn together, Rembrandt painted a second portrait of Alexander and sent it to Sicily. And when Ruffo found the work unfinished, he happily did more work on it and returned it to Ruffo.

The Death of Rembrandt's Second Companion

The proceeds from his work for the Sicilian collector did not solve Rembrandt's financial problems. On 27 October 1662 he was forced to sell Saskia's tomb in the Oudekerk. The one he bought in the Westerkerk, a church at the end of the Rozengracht, was no doubt cheaper.

The will Hendrickje had made on 7 August 1661 when she was ill, giving Rembrandt a life interest in her estate, of which their daughter Cornelia was the legal heiress, could not have provided him much security. It testified, however, to the close relationship between them.

Like Saskia, in a comparable deed drawn up by a notary in 1642, Hendrickje is termed *juffrouw* (madam) and *huisvrouw* (spouse). Did Rembrandt and Hendrickje marry? While it is possible, there is no proof. For years Rembrandt had refused to do so in order not to forfeit his claims on Saskia's estate. Then debt and bankruptcy won the day. What Hendrickje left when she died at the end of July 1663 was laughable. She was buried in the Westerkerk, where Saskia's remains now lay.

R embrandt painted *Aristotle Contemplating the Bust of Homer* (below) in 1653 for a rich Sicilian collector who had commissioned a portrait of a philosopher. Aristotle, poet, philosopher, and tutor and friend of Alexander the Great, had the added virtue in Rembrandt's eyes of being a warrior. Adorned by a medallion of Alexander, the

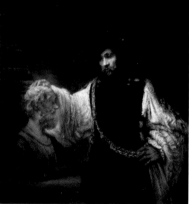

philosopher is shown resting his hand on the head of a bust of the blind poet Homer. The bust of Alexander on the medallion and Rembrandt's portrait *Alexander the Great* (right), painted in 1663, were inspired by the same image of an armed and helmeted Pallas Athena.

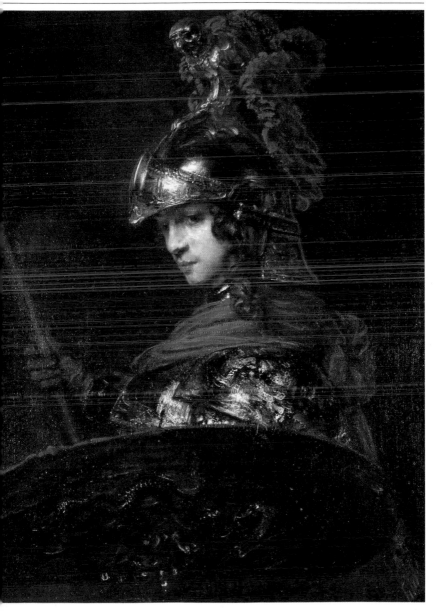

Titus, Only Twenty-One, Was Left to House, Feed, and Help Rembrandt on His Own

Rembrandt was driven to borrow again, twice from Harmen Becker. This dealer in precious stones and textiles was also a collector. He already owned several works by Rembrandt and was happy to lend money to destitute artists, accepting a painting as guarantee. When after some months Rembrandt thought he had settled all debts with Becker, it transpired that the latter had taken over from Lodewijk van Ludick the entitlement to repayment which he, in turn, had purchased from Jan Six. It was not money so much as a painting that Becker expected from Rembrandt. The subject he requested was Juno.

By spring 1664 Becker was growing impatient. The Juno was still unfinished. Why the delay? Possibly Rembrandt was busy with a commission from Frederick Rihel for an equestrian portrait commemorating his role in William III's honor guard when he entered Amsterdam in 1660. Perhaps he was painting a portrait of Titus.

At the beginning of 1665 one of Rembrandt's creditors, Isaac van Heertsbeeck, was obliged by law to return to Titus, as a privileged creditor, the proceeds he had received from the sale of Rembrandt's chattels. Titus received another 6952 guilders from the sale of the house on the Breestraat.

He must have given the money directly to his father. How else could Rembrandt have offered 1000 guilders for a painting by Hans Holbein the Younger? Rembrandt did not contemplate buying the house in which he now lived on the Rozengracht—the owner had recently died—but he continued to buy works of art.

On 29 December 1667 Cosimo III de' Medici, Future Grand Duke of Tuscany, Visited Rembrandt in His House on the Rozengracht

Filippo Corsini, who was accompanying him, recorded in his diary: "Thursday 29 [December] early, the day was fine but cold, and the sky clouded over around five

A rich merchant from Strasbourg, Frederick Rihel was one of 108 mounted guards who escorted the ten-year-old William III on his entry into the city of Amsterdam in 1660. It was this instant of glory that he wanted immortalized in the life-size portrait *Frederick Rihel on Horseback* (right). Equestrian portraits are a rarity in Dutch art. Indeed, in the case of Rembrandt, this one is unique, if *The Polish Rider* is taken to be by another hand. (Rembrandt had in 1655 drawn *The Skeleton Rider*, in which he rendered both man and horse in skeletal form.) To paint an equestrian portrait, however, meant inviting comparison with Titian's *Charles V* and Roman statues; hence no doubt the almost hieratic stiffness of the horse, reinforcing the rider's air of importance. Illuminated in the background, the royal carriage and the young prince can be glimpsed in profile.

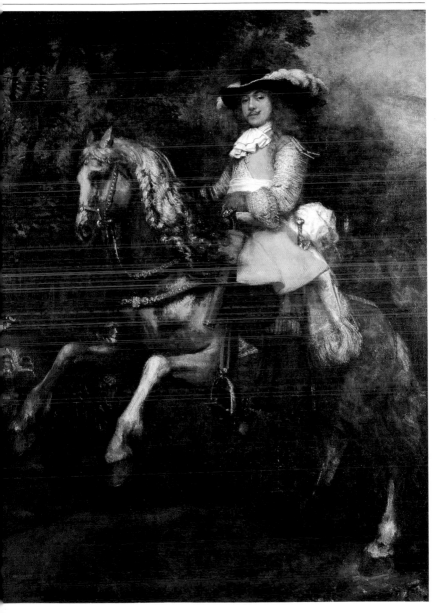

o'clock in the afternoon, since, as is typical of the climate, fog gathered and hung around until night, which is normally calm. His Highness, after attending mass, went with Blaeu and Ferroni to look at paintings by various masters, among them the designer Wan Welde, Reinbrent the famous painter, Scamus who does seascapes, and others who did not have finished paintings, so that we visited private homes where we could look at their works. His Highness went and was greeted in the warmest and most respectful manner."

What paintings would Cosimo have seen in the house of "Reinbrent the famous painter"? Unfinished portraits, perhaps: a thickset old man whose fists grip the arms of an armchair; sketches for a pair of portraits of a man and a woman, he with his thumb upon a pair of gloves, her hand upon the handle of a fan; and self-portraits. Cosimo certainly bought one for his collection. Cardinal Leopoldo de' Medici had early in the century started a collection of self-portraits by famous painters, modeled on existing collections of portraits of famous men. After the cardinal's death, responsibility for this collection passed into the hands

R aphael's *Self-Portrait* (below left) bears the marks of his Florentine sojourn and Leonardo's influence. On 28 October 1682 it became part of the collection of Cardinal Leopoldo de' Medici (1617–75), who wanted to create a collection of self-portraits of painters.

R ubens' *Self-Portrait* (below right) was given to Cosimo III de' Medici in 1713 by Johann Wilhelm von der Pfalz, Elector Palatine of the Rhine. The Grand Dukes of Tuscany continued the collection until the unification of Italy at the end of the 19th century.

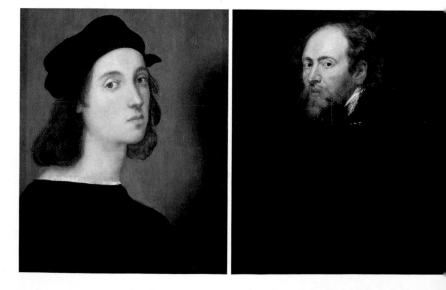

of the grand duke. How could a portrait of this "famous painter" have been passed over?

What Did Cosimo, on His European Tour, and Rembrandt, Who Had Never Left His Homeland, Say to Each Other?

"He dissuaded his visitors from looking at his works too closely, saying to each one: 'The smell of the paint will displease you.'" Rembrandt did not give this advice (recounted by Houbraken) to Cosimo. The exchanges between the two men, being dictated by protocol, no doubt involved a rendering of homage and a paying of respects. Might Cosimo have seen the first stage of a portrait of a couple, or even the finished work, in the house on the Rozengracht? The illegible date on the canvas leaves us uncertain.

The man's left hand is placed over the shoulder of the young woman standing at his side (see next page). His right hand, which she touches with her left, rests on her breast. Who were the models for this tender, serene, and voluptuous portrait? The love of Jacob and Rachel, or Isaac and Rebecca? Was it Titus with the young woman

The *Self-Portrait* of Velázquez (below left) was bought in Spain in 1689 by Cosimo da Castiglione for the collection of the Grand Dukes of Tuscany. Velázquez, who was court painter to Philip IV, is carrying the keys of the Usher of the Chamber office at his waist.

The *Self-Portrait* of Rembrandt (below right) was probably the one bought by Cosimo III de' Medici when he was visiting Amsterdam. Today it hangs in the Uffizi, in Florence.

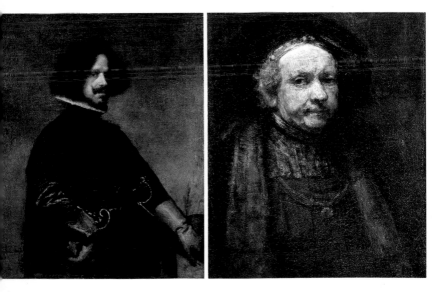

he married on 10 February 1668, Magdalena van Loo, the daughter of the silversmith Jan van Loo? We can only speculate on the models for *The Jewish Bride* (a title which, like others, was not given by Rembrandt).

The Painter as One of the Myths of Antiquity

The poet Jeremias de Decker claimed that Rembrandt was the "Apelles of his time," "excellent and universally known." (Apelles was a 4th century BC Greek painter.) In the early 1630s Constantijn Huygens had written that Rembrandt surpassed Protogenes, Apelles, and Parrhasius.

However, it was with none of these painters from antiquity, painters who were legends, models, beacons, painters of whom nothing remained, that Rembrandt chose to identify himself. Instead he decided to associate

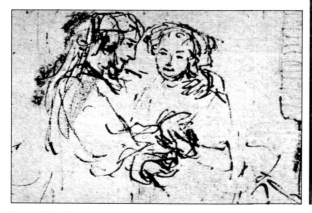

himself with Zeuxis, because of the particular circumstances of Zeuxis' death.

Zeuxis, celebrated Greek artist of the 5th century BC, was visited by an old woman who commissioned an Aphrodite from him. The painter accepted the commission. The old woman then demanded that she herself should be the model. At one of the sittings the painter burst out laughing on viewing the portrait and the model. And in the end he died laughing. Was there in Rembrandt's studio a portrait of himself, bursting with mirth, in front of a faded portrait of a woman?

Many attempts have been made to identify the subject of this 1665 painting, known as *The Jewish Bride* (drawing left). Who is the woman? What mattered to Rembrandt was not his subject so much as the feelings it elicited. Amid the rich color he created a feeling of joy and gentleness.

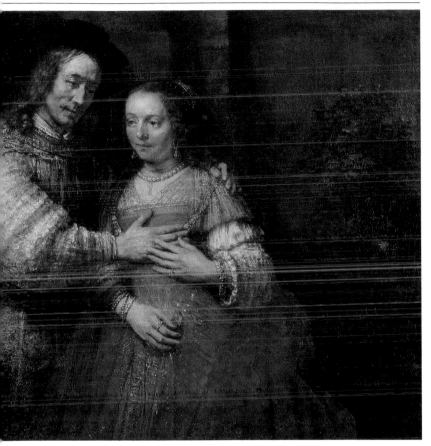

Rembrandt, Worn Out, Wrinkled, and Bloated from Gin, Contemplated His Models

The demands of the models, the demands of painting—Rembrandt laughed, but it was grim laughter.

He was on his own. Alone with a fifteen-year-old daughter. "He lived very simply, often making do at meals with a little bread and cheese or smoked herring." (This detail comes from Arnold Houbraken, who talked to a number of people who had known Rembrandt.) Titus, following his marriage to Magdalena van Loo,

Rembrandt used a knife to apply the gold on the man's sleeve, its relief creating shadow. In places the paint is scraped and polished to give the material an almost tactile aspect, as inviting to the touch as it is to the eye.

lived in his mother-in-law's house on the Singelgracht.

On 4 September 1668 Titus died. He was buried in the Westerkerk. On 22 March 1669 his daughter, Titia, was baptized in the Nieuwe Zijdeskapel.

Rembrandt painted the group portrait of a family, and his own grief-stricken smile, again and again; he also painted *Simeon and the Child Jesus in the Temple*, which the painter Allart van Everdingen and his son Cornelis would see in Rembrandt's studio in September 1669.

R embrandt painted *The Ruin* (below) in 1650. His *A Family Group* (below left) was probably realized in the last year of his life. Opposite: A drawing of the Westerkerk, where Rembrandt and his family were buried. Overleaf: *Self-Portrait* (1665).

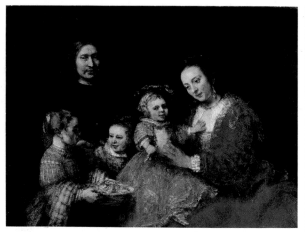

On 4 October 1669 Rembrandt Died, at the Age of Sixty-Three

The pictures were turned against the wall. The mirrors were covered in black crepe, as tradition dictated. On 8 October Rembrandt was buried in the Westerkerk, next to Hendrickje and Titus. There was no official notice of his death. Only the church register recorded the fact: "8 October. Rembrandt van Rijn, painter, living on the Rozengracht, opposite Doolhof, coffin with six bearers; leaves two children. Costs charged: twenty guilders."

A few days after his death an inventory of Rembrandt's effects was drawn up. It was necessary to determine what was to go to Cornelia and what to Titia, who would inherit under the terms of Rembrandt's formal agreement with Hendrickje and Titus. The inventory of the house in Sint Anthoniesdijk on the Breestraat had listed 363 items. Some fifty covered the inventory of the contents of the house on the Rozengracht: furniture, linen, crockery, paintings, drawings—and of course curios, weapons, pieces of armor, antiques. Ruined and forsaken, Rembrandt had not ceased (as Baldinucci had written) to collect things "he thought might be of use to a painter."

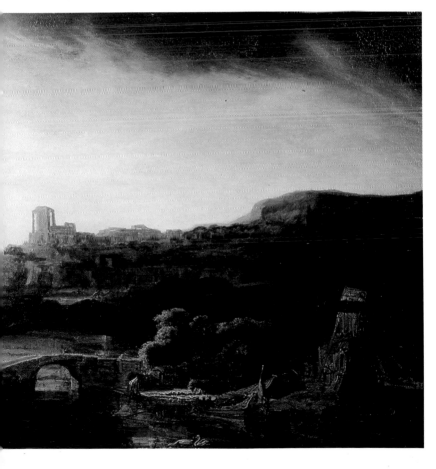

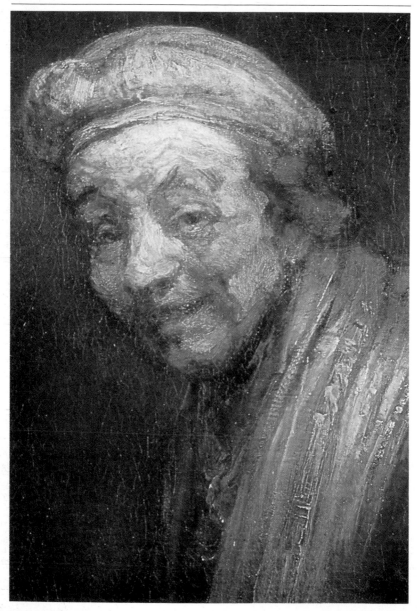

DOCUMENTS

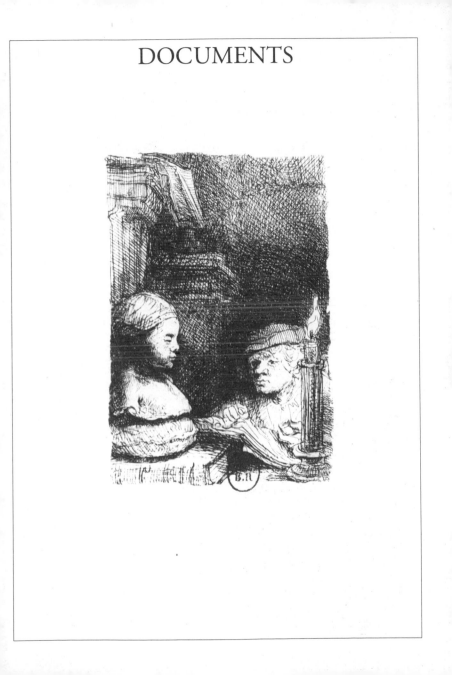

From Rembrandt's House

This is the inventory compiled on 25–6 July 1656 of Rembrandt's paintings, furniture, and other effects from his house in Sint Anthoniesdijk on the Breestraat.

The front of the house was altered in the 18th century.

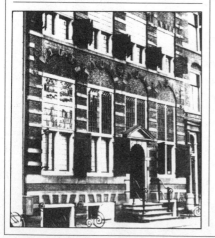

In the Entrance Hall

1. A small piece by Ad. Brouwer, representing a pastry cook
2. 1…of gamblers by the same Brouwer
3. 1…of a woman with child by Rembrandt
4. A painter's studio by the same Brouwer
5. A fancy spread of food by the same Brouwer
6. A plaster head
7. 2 naked children in plaster
8. A sleeping child in plaster
9. A shabby shoe
10. A small landscape by Rembrandt
11. Another landscape by the same
12. A small standing figure by the same
13. A candlelight scene by Jan Lievens
14. A *St. Jerome* by Rembrandt
15. A small painting of hares by the same
16. A small painting of a hog by the same
17. A small landscape by Hercules Seghers
18. A landscape by Jan Lievensz
19. Another one by the same
20. A small landscape by Rembrandt
21. *Fighting Lions* by the same
22. A *Moonlight Scene* by Jan Lievensz
23. A portrait head by Rembrandt
24. A portrait head by the same
25. A still life retouched by Rembrandt
26. A *Soldier in Armor* by the same
27. A *Vanitas* retouched by Rembrandt
28. Another one with a scepter, retouched
29. A seascape completed by Hendrick Antonisz
30. 4 Spanish chairs with Russian leather
31. 2 chairs with black seats
32. A stepstool made of pine

In the Antechamber

33. A painting of the Samaritan, retouched by Rembrandt
34. A *Rich Man* by Palma Vecchio, of which Pieter de la Tombe owns a half share
35. A *Shed* by Rembrandt
36. 2 greyhounds from life by the same
37. A large *Descent from the Cross* by

Rembrandt, with a handsome gold frame by the same

38. A *Raising of Lazarus* by the same
39. A *Courtesan Doing Her Hair,* by the same
40. A wooded landscape by Hercules Seghers
41. A *Tobias* by Lastman
42. A *Raising of Lazarus* by Jan Lievensz
43. A small mountain landscape by Rembrandt
44. A small landscape by Govaert Jansz
45. 2 portrait heads by Rembrandt
46. A grisaille by Jan Lievensz
47. 2 grisailles by Porcellis
48. A portrait head by Rembrandt
49. Another one by Brouwer
50. A view from the dunes by Porcellis
51. A smaller one of the same by the same
52. A small hermit by Jan Lievensz
53. 2 small portrait heads by Lucas van Valckenburgh
54. A *Burning Camp* by the elder Bassano
55. *A Quacksalver,* after Brouwer
56. 2 heads by Jan Pynas
57. A perspective view by Lucas van Leyden
58. A priest after Jan Lievensz
59. A small study of a model by Rembrandt
60. A small herding scene by the same
61. A drawing by the same
62. A *Flagellation of Christ* by the same
63. A grisaille by Porcellis
64. A grisaille by Simon de Vlieger
65. A small landscape by Rembrandt
66. A portrait head painted from life by Rembrandt
67. A portrait head by Raphael of Urbino
68. Some houses from life by Rembrandt
69. A landscape from nature by the same
70. Some small houses by Hercules Seghers
71. A *Juno* by Pynas
72. A mirror in an ebony frame
73. An ebony frame
74. A marble [wine-] cooling bucket
75. A walnut table with a *tournai* cloth
76. 7 Spanish chairs with green velvet seats

In the Room Behind the Antechamber

77. A painting of Jephta
78. A *Virgin with Child* by Rembrandt
79. A *Crucifixion of Christ,* designed by the same
80. A *Naked Woman* by the same
81. A copy after Annibale Carracci
82. 2 figures in half-length by Brouwer
83. Another copy after Annibale Caracci
84. A small seascape by Porcellis
85. A head of an old man by van Eyck
86. A portrait of the deceased by Abraham Vinck
87. A *Resurrection of the Dead* by Aertie van Leyden
88. A sketch by Rembrandt
89. A copy after a sketch by Rembrandt
90. 2 portrait heads from life by Rembrandt
91. *The Consecration of Solomon's Temple* in grisaille by the same
92. The *Christ's Circumcision,* copy after Rembrandt
93. 2 small landscapes by Hercules Seghers
94. A gilded frame
95. A small oak table
96. 4 cardboard shades [or screens]
97. An oak press
98. 4 plain chairs
99. 4 green chair cushions
100. A copper kettle
101. A coatrack

In the Room Behind the Parlor

102. A wooded landscape by an unknown master
103. A head of an old man by Rembrandt
104. A large landscape by Hercules Seg[h]ers
105. A head of a woman by Rembrandt
106. The *Concord of the State* by the same
107. A *Small Village* by Govaert Jansz
108. A *Small Ox* from life by Rembrandt
109. A large picture of *The Samaritan Woman* by Giorgione, of which a half share belongs to Pieter [de] la Tombe
110. 3 antique statues

111. A sketch of *Christ's Entombment* by Rembrandt
112. A *St. Peter's Boat* by Aertie van Leyden
113. A *Christ's Resurrection* by Rembrandt
114. A figure of the Virgin by Raphael of Urbino
115. A *Head of Christ* by Rembrandt
116. A small winter scene by Grimmer
117. The *Crucifixion of Christ* by Lelio da Novellara
118. A *Head of Christ* by Rembrandt
119. A small ox, by Las[t]man
120. A *Vanitas* retouched by Rembrandt
121. An *Ecce Homo* in grisaille by Rembrandt
122. An *Abraham's Sacrifice* by Jan Lievensz
123. A *Vanitas* retouched by Rembrandt
124. A landscape, in grisaille, by Hercules Seghers
125. *Sunset* by Rembrandt
126. A large mirror
127. 6 chairs with blue seats
128. An oak table
129. An embroidered table cloth
130. A cedar press
131. A cupboard of the same [wood]
132. A bed and bolster
133. 2 pillows
134. 2 blankets
135. A blue hanging
136. A wicker chair
137. A warming pan

In the Art Chamber

138. 2 terrestrial globes
139. A small box of minerals
140. A small column
141. A small pewter pot
142. A urinating child
143. 2 East Indian cups
144. A bowl…with a little Chinaman
145. A sculpture of an empress
146. An East Indian powder box
147. A sculpture of the Emperor Augustus
148. An Indian cup
149. A sculpture of Tiberius
150. An East Indian sewing box
151. A head of Caius
152. A Caligula
153. 2 porcelain cassowaries
154. A Heraclitus
155. 2 porcelain figurines
156. A Nero
157. 2 iron helmets
158. A Japanese helmet
159. A Croatian helmet
160. A Roman emperor
161. A moor['s head] cast from life
162. A Socrates
163. A Homer
164. An Aristotle
165. A burnished antique head
166. A Faustina
167. An iron armor and helmet
168. An emperor Galba
169. An…Otto
170. An…Vitellus
171. An…Vespasian
172. A Titus Vespasian
173. An…Domitian
174. An…Silius Brutus
175. 47 specimens of land and sea animals and the like
176. 23 sea and land animals
177. 1 net with two calabashes, one made of copper
178. 8 plaster casts from life, large

On the Shelf in the Back

179. A great quantity of shells, coral branches, casts from life…
180. A figure of an antique Cupid
181. A handgun, a pistol
182. An old ornamented iron shield made by Quentin the Smith
183. An old-fashioned powder horn
184. A Turkish powder horn
185. A cabinet with medals
186. A padded shield
187. 2 completely nude figures
188. A deathmask of Prince Maurice, cast from his own face
189. A lion and a bull modeled from life

190. Several walking sticks

191. A longbow

The Art Books

192. A book of sketches by Rembrandt

193. A book of woodcuts by Van Leyden

194. The same with woodcuts by Wael....

195. 1...with copper plate engravings by Vanni and others including Barocci

196. 1...with copperplate engravings by Raphael of Urbino

197. A small gilt bedstead modeled by Verhulst

198. 1...with copper engravings by Lucas van Leyden including duplicates and single sheets

199. 1...with drawings by the leading masters of the entire world

200. The precious book of Andrea Mantegna

201. 1...of large size filled with drawings and prints by many masters

202. Another...of larger size with drawings and prints by various masters

203. 1...filled with curious drawings in miniature as well as woodcuts and engravings on copper of various costumes

204. 1...with prints by the elder Breughel

205. 1...with prints by Raphael of Urbino

206. 1...with very precious prints by the same

207. 1...filled with prints by Antonio Tempesta

208. 1...with copperplate engravings and woodcuts by Lucas Cranach

209. 1...of Annibale, Agostino, and Ludovico Carracci, Guido Reni, and Spagnaletto

210. 1...with engraved and etched figures by Antonio Tempesta

211. 1...a large book of the same

212. 1...book, as above

213. 1...with engraved copperplate prints of portraits by Goltzius and Muller

214. 1...with very fine impressions [of prints] by Raphael of Urbino

215. 1...with drawings by Ad. Brouwer

216. 1...very large, with almost all the work of Titian

217. A few rare items of pottery and of Venetian glass

218. 1 antique book with a series of sketches by Rembrandt

219. An antique book

220. A large book filled with sketches by Rembrandt

221. Another antique book, empty

222. A small backgammon board

223. An antique chair...

224. A Chinese bowl containing minerals

225. A large lump of white coral

226. A book filled with copperplate engravings of statues

227. 1...with all the works of Heemskerck

228. A book filled with portraits, of van Dyck, Rubens, and other old masters

229. 1...full of landscapes by various masters

230. 1...full of the work of Michelangelo Buonarroti

231. 2 woven baskets

232. 1...with erotica by Raphael, Rosso, Annibale Carracci, and Giulio Bonasone

233. 1...full of landscapes by various esteemed masters

234. 1...full of Turkish buildings by Melchior Lorck, Hendrick Coeck van Aelst, and others, depicting Turkish life

235. 1 East Indian basket containing various prints by Rembrandt, Hollar, Cock, and others

236. A book bound in black leather with the best sketches by Rembrandt

237. A cardboard box with prints of Schongauer, Holbein, Hans Brosamer, and Israel van Meeckenem

238. Another book with all of Rembrandt's works

239. A book filled with drawings by Rembrandt of nude men and women

240. 1 book filled with drawings of all Roman buildings and views by all the most excellent masters

241. A Chinese basket full of portrait casts
242. An empty album
243. 1…as above
244. 1 ditto, full of landscapes drawn by Rembrandt from nature
245. 1…with trial proofs by Rubens and Jacob Jordaens
246. 1…full of portraits by Mierevelt, Titian, and others
247. A small Chinese basket
248. 1…filled with prints of architecture
249. 1…filled with drawings by Rembrandt of animals done from life
250. 1…full of prints by Frans Floris, Buytewech, Goltzius, and Abraham Bloemart
251. A packet of drawings from the antique by Rembrandt
252. 5 small books in quarto, filled with drawings by Rembrandt
253. 1…with drawings of architecture
254. *Medea,* tragedy by Jan Six
255. *All of Jerusalem* by Jacques Callot
256. A book in vellum filled with landscapes drawn from nature by Rembrandt
257. 1…filled with figure sketches by Rembrandt
257a. 1…as above
258. A small book with wooden covers with [sketches of] circular plates
259. A small book containing views by Rembrandt
260. 1…with outstanding calligraphy
261. 1…full of drawings of statues by Rembrandt done from life
262. 1…as above
263. 1…full of sketches by Las[t]man in pen [and ink]
264. 1…by Las[t]man in red chalk
265. 1…with sketches by Rembrandt done in pen
266. 1…as above
267. 1…as before
268. Another one…by the same
269. Another one…by the same
270. 1…large, with drawings of the Tyrol by Roelant Savery drawn from nature

271. 1…full of drawings by various eminent masters
272. 1…in quarto, filled with sketches by Rembrandt
273. The book on proportion with woodcuts by Albrecht Dürer
274. Another engraved book [album] with prints comprising the works of Jan Lievensz and Ferdinand Bol
275. A few packets of sketches…
276. A stack of paper of very large size
277. A box of prints by van Vliet after paintings by Rembrandt
278. A cloth room divider
279. An iron gorget
280. A drawer in which there is a bird of paradise and 6 fans
281. 15 books of various sizes
282. A book in High German with military figures
283. 1…with woodcuts
284. A *Flavius Josephus* in High German profusely illustrated by Tobias Stimmer
285. An old Bible
286. A small marble inkstand
287. The plaster cast of Prince Maurice

In the Antechamber of the Art Room

288. A *Joseph* by Aertie van Leyden
289. 3 framed prints
290. *The Annunciation*
291. A small landscape painted from nature by Rembrandt
292. A small landscape by Hercules Seghers
293. The *Descent from the Cross* by Rembrandt
294. A head, from life
295. A death's head, painted over by Rembrandt
296. A *Diana Bathing,* in plaster by Adam van Vianen
297. A model, from life, by Rembrandt
298. 3 little dogs…by Titus van Rijn
299. A painted book by the same
300. A *Head of the Virgin* by the same
301. A small landscape in moonlight, overpainted by Rembrandt

302. A copy of *Christ's Flagellation* after Rembrandt

303. A small nude woman, done from life by Rembrandt

304. A small unfinished landscape, from nature, by the same

305. A horse, from nature, by the same

306. A small picture by the young Hals

307. A small fish, from life

308. A bowl, modeled in plaster, with nude figures, by Adam van Vianen

309. An old trunk

310. 4 chairs with black leather seats

311. A pine table

In the Small Studio

312. 33 pieces of antique hand weapons and wind instruments

313. 60 pieces of Indian hand weapons, arrows, shafts, javelins, and bows

314. 13 pieces of bamboo wind instruments

315. 13 pieces of arrows, bows, shields, etc.

316. A large quantity of hands and heads cast from life, together with a harp and a Turkish bow

317. 17 hands and arms, cast from life

318. A quantity of antlers

319. 4 crossbows and footbows

320. 5 antique helmets and shields

321. 9 gourds and bottles

322. 2 sculpted heads of Barthold Been and his wife

323. A plaster cast of a Greek antique

324. A statue of the Emperor Agrippa

325. ...of the Emperor Aurelius

326. A head of Christ, a study from life

327. A satyr's head with horns

328. An antique Sibyl

329. An antique Laocoön

330. A large sea plant

331. A Vitellius

332. A Seneca

333. 3 or 4 antique heads of women

334. Another 4 different heads

335. A small metal cannon

336. A quantity of ancient textiles of various colors

337. 7 stringed instruments

338. 2 small paintings by Rembrandt

In the Large Studio

339. 20 pieces, including halberds, swords, and Indian fans

340. Costumes for an Indian man and woman

341. A giant's head

342. 5 cuirasses

343. A wooden trumpet

344. 2 Moors in a picture by Rembrandt

345. A little child by Michelangelo Buonarroti

On the Picture Rack

346. The skins of a lion and a lioness with 2 multicolored coats

347. A large picture of Danae

348. A bittern from life, by Rembrandt

In the Small Office

349. 10 pieces, small and large paintings, by Rembrandt

350. A bedstead

In the Small Kitchen

351. A pewter water jug

352. Several pots and pans

353. A small table

354. A cupboard

355. Several old chairs

356. 2 seat cushions

In the Hallway

357. 9 white bowls

358. 2 earthenware dishes

Linen at the Laundry

359. 3 men's shirts

360. 6 handkerchiefs

361. 12 napkins

362. 3 tablecloths

363. A few collars and cuffs

Marjon van der Meulen and
Walter L. Strauss (eds.),
The Rembrandt Documents, 1979

Rembrandt and His Contemporaries

Rembrandt's exceptional ability was recognized early on. These passages give an insight into the reactions of a contemporary connoisseur and a pupil.

R embrandt, *Judas Returning the Thirty Pieces of Silver* (detail), 1629.

"Praise and Hail to You"

Constantijn Huygens, private secretary to the stadtholder, was a great admirer of Rembrandt's art. His diary, written in 1631 in Latin, contains one of the earliest and most enthusiastic descriptions of the young painter's work.

His picture of Judas repenting, who brings back to the High Priest the pieces of silver, the reward for his treason to Our Lord, can, in my opinion, stand comparison with any work of art. Let the whole of Italy attempt to compete with that picture as well as anything beautiful or admirable that has come down from the earliest times. Setting aside the many figures contained in that single canvas, I would like to draw attention to one figure—that of Judas in his despair: his face tortured by fear, in convulsions of rage, begging, craving for remission, and yet with not a gleam of hope, his hair tousled, his garments in rags, his arms

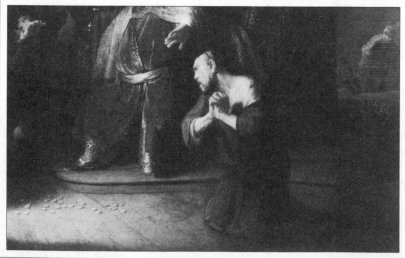

distorted, his hands twisted until the blood flows, flinging himself frantically on his knees, his whole body bent in miserable suffering—all that I would like to contrast with the elegance of our men of the world, and then even the most ignorant of all mortal men would understand, that antiquity has not produced anything comparable either in poetry or painting. For I would claim that neither Protogenes, nor Apelles, nor Parrhasius could have conceived, nor would be able to conceive even if they could come back to life, such a wealth of special and general features—I tremble in writing this down!—as this Dutch son of a miller in his single figure. Praise and hail to you, my Rembrandt! Neither Troy nor the whole of Asia have brought so much high fame to Italy as Italy and Greece together have brought to the Netherlands—in the person of a young Dutchman who has scarcely ever been beyond the bounds of his hometown, let alone his country.

Diary of Constantijn Huygens
From Richard Friedenthal
Letters of the Great Artists, 1963

The Master's Methods

From a 1686 account by one of Rembrandt's pupils, Bernhardt Keil.

This painter, different in his mental makeup from other people as regards self-control, was also most extravagant in his style of painting and evolved for himself a manner which may be called entirely his own, that is, without contour or limitation by means of inner and outer lines, but entirely consisting of violent and repeated strokes, with great strength of darks after his own fashion, but without any profound darks. And that which is almost impossible to understand is this: how, painting by means of these strokes, he worked so slowly, and completed his things with a tardiness and toil never equaled by anybody. He could have painted a great number of portraits, owing to the great prestige which in those parts had been gained by his coloring, to which his drawing did not, however, come up; but after it had become commonly known that whoever wanted to be portrayed by him had to sit to him for some two or three months, there were few who came forward. The cause of his slowness was that, immediately after the first work had dried, he took it up again, repainting it with bigger or smaller strokes, so that at times the pigment in a given place was raised more than half the thickness of a finger. Hence it may be said of him that he always toiled without rest, painted much, and completed very few pictures.... This extravagance of manner was entirely consistent with Rembrandt's mode of living, since he was a most temperamental man and despised everyone. The ugly and plebeian face with which he was ill-favored was accompanied by untidy and dirty clothes, since it was his custom, when working, to wipe his brushes on himself, and to do other things of a similar nature. When he worked he would not have granted an audience to the first monarch in the world, who would have had to return and return again until he had found him no longer engaged upon that work.

Filippo Baldinucci,
From *Rembrandt: Selected Paintings*,
Introduction and notes by
Tancred Borenius, 1942

Two Painters Look at Rembrandt

Over the centuries artists continued to look on Rembrandt as a master. His work was a point of reference, a challenge, an enigma.

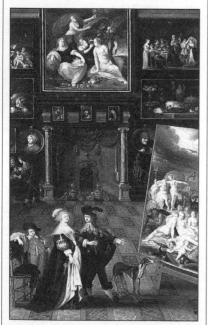

I*nterior of a Gallery of Pictures and Objets d'Art* by Cornelis de Brellieur.

The Benefit of Exaggeration: Eugène Delacroix Observes the Work of Rembrandt

6 June 1851

Although it is necessary to take account of all the parts of the figure, so as not to misrepresent the proportions that clothing may hide, I do not think one should subscribe exclusively to this method, as he always seems scrupulously to have done, to judge by the studies by him which remain.

I am very sure that if Rembrandt had confined himself to this studio practice he would not have achieved either the theatrical power or the mastery of effects that make his pictures such true renderings of nature. Perhaps Rembrandt will prove in the long run to be a far greater painter than Raphael.

I write this blasphemy, calculated to horrify every right-thinking student of painting, without wanting to make an issue of it; it is only that the more I progress through life, the more I am inwardly convinced that truth is what is most beautiful and most rare. What Rembrandt lacks, if you will, is the absolute elevation of Raphael.

Perhaps that elevation which Raphael has in the lines, in the majesty of each of his figures, Rembrandt has in his mysterious conception of his subjects, in the deep naturalness of their expressions and gestures. Although one may prefer the majestic emphasis of Raphael, which is perhaps suited to the grandeur of certain subjects, one can reasonably claim, without inviting the derision of men of taste, and I mean genuine and sincere taste, that the great Dutchman was more instinctively a painter than the studious pupil of Perugino.

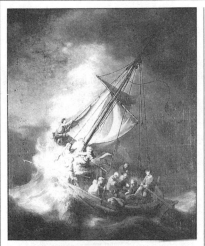

The Storm on the Sea of Galilee (1633), the only seascape by Rembrandt.

28 April 1853

It takes a multitude of *sacrifices* to get the maximum effect in painting, and I believe I make a good many, but I can't bear it when the artist shows his hand. There are notwithstanding very fine things that have been conceived to produce an extreme effect, among them the works of Rembrandt and our native [Alexandre Gabriel] Decamps [1803–60]. Exaggeration is natural to them and not at all shocking in their case. I make this reflection as I look at my portrait of M. Bruyas; Rembrandt would have concentrated on the head; the hands would have been barely indicated, likewise the clothing. Without saying that I prefer the method which presents all objects to the eye according to their degree of importance—for I admire Rembrandt exceedingly—I feel that I should manage clumsily in attempting those effects. I am on the side of the Italians in this. Paul Veronese is the *ne plus ultra* of rendering, in all parts of the picture; the same is true of Rubens, and perhaps he has the advantage over the glorious Paolo when it comes to pathos, in that he knows how to draw attention to the principal object by selective exaggerations, thus intensifying the expressive force of his work. On the other hand there is something artificial in this manner, which one feels as much or perhaps even more than the sacrifices in Rembrandt's work, and the vagueness that he employs in such a marked way in the less important areas. Neither alternative satisfies me when it comes to my own case.

What I want—and I believe I often encounter it—is that artifice should be barely perceptible, and that the object of interest should nonetheless be properly singled out; something which can once again only be achieved by sacrifices; however, these need to be infinitely more subtle than those found in Rembrandt's work to accord with my taste.

5 July 1854

It is really only with Rembrandt that one begins to see in pictures a harmony between the accessory features and the main subject, to my mind one of the most important things.... On this subject one could compare the work of the masters.

29 July 1854

The landscapes of Titian, of Rembrandt, and of Poussin are, as a rule, in harmony with the figures. In the case of Rembrandt himself—and he carries this to perfection—the background and the figures are absolutely one. Interest is everywhere: you do not isolate any part, any more than when contemplating a beautiful scene in nature, where everything contributes to your delight....

When copying a [work by] Titian or Rembrandt we think that we are rendering the relationship of light and shade in the same terms as the master; we religiously reproduce the work or, rather, the ravages worked on it by time. The great men would be very painfully surprised to come upon smoky daubs instead of their works as they actually painted them.

29 October 1857

One does not generally find in French painting any of that felicitous neglect of detail which has the merit of drawing the attention to the parts that deserve it. The Flemish excel in this, not to mention Rembrandt, in whom this feature is as much the product of calculation as of instinct, his capricious etching needle committing itself to no more than a superficial rendering, even in the essential parts. One notices in the works of the Dutch and the Flemish, in their paintings as in their engravings, an ease of execution, an artful concealment of sacrifices that captures the imagination.

Eugène Delacroix
Journal, 1822–63

Van Gogh's Reactions

18 September 1877

So, having some leisure, I could carry out an old plan to go to see the etchings by Rembrandt in the Trippenhuis; I went there this morning, and am glad I did. While there, I thought, Couldn't Theo and I see them together someday? Think about whether you could spare a day or two for such things. How would a man like Father, who so often goes

long distances, even in the night with a lantern, to visit a sick or dying man, to speak with him about One whose word is a light even in the night of suffering and agony—how would he feel about Rembrandt's etchings, for instance, *The Flight into Egypt in the Night* or the *Burial of Jesus?* The collection in the

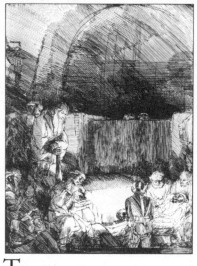

T*he Entombment,* a 1654 etching.

Trippenhuis is splendid....

Blessed twilight, when two or three are gathered in His name and He is in the midst of them, and blessed is he who knows these things and follows them, too.

Rembrandt knew that, for from the rich treasure of his heart he produced, among other things, that drawing in sepia, charcoal, ink, etc., which is in the British Museum representing the house in Bethany. In that room twilight has fallen; the figure of our Lord, noble and impressive, stands out serious and dark against the window, which the evening twilight is filtering through. At Jesus' feet sits Mary who has chosen the good part, which shall not be taken away from her; Martha is in the room busy with something or other—if I remember correctly, she is stirring the fire, or something like that. I hope I forget neither that drawing nor what it seems to say to me: "I am the light of the world: He that followeth me shall not walk in darkness, but shall have the light of life."

30 October 1877

I cannot sit up so late in the evening any more—uncle has strictly forbidden it. Still, I keep in mind the phrase under the etching by Rembrandt, *"In medio noctis vim suam lux exerit"* (In the middle of the night, the light diffuses its strength), and I keep a small gaslight burning low all night; *"in medio noctis"* I often lie looking at it, planning my work for the next day and thinking of how to arrange my studies best.

I hope to light the fire early in the morning this winter, the winter mornings have something peculiar about them.

October 1885

The Syndics [see pp. 116–7] is perfect, is the most beautiful Rembrandt; but *The Jewish Bride* [above right]—not ranked so high—what an intimate, what an infinitely sympathetic picture it is, painted *d'une main de feu*. You see, in *The Syndics* Rembrandt is true to nature, though *even there*, and always, he soars aloft, to the very highest height, the infinite; but Rembrandt could do more than that—if he did not have to be *literally* true, as in a portrait, when he was free to *idealize*, to be poet, that means Creator. That's what he is in *The Jewish Bride*. How Delacroix

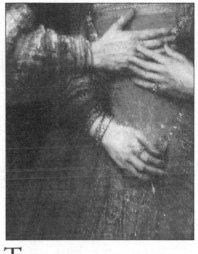

The *Jewish Bride* (detail), c. 1668.

would have understood that picture. What a noble sentiment, infinitely deep. *Il faut être mort plusieurs fois pour peindre ainsi* [One must have died several times to paint like that], how true it is here. As to the pictures by Frans Hals—he always remains on *earth*—one can speak about them. Rembrandt is so deeply mysterious that he says things for which there are no words in any language. Rembrandt is truly called *magician*…that's not an easy calling.

October 1885

I have especially admired the hands by Rembrandt and Hals, certain hands in *The Syndics*, even in *The Jewish Bride* and in Frans Hals, hands that lived, but were not finished in the sense they demand nowadays.

October 1885

The fragment, Rembrandt's *Lesson in Anatomy*, yes, I was absolutely staggered

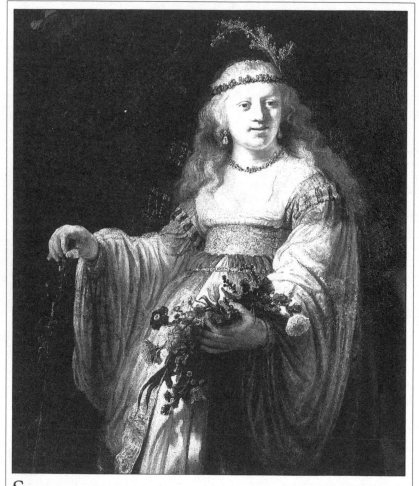

*S*askia as Flora (1635).

by that too. Do you remember those flesh colors—it is—*de la terre*—especially the feet [see p. 99].

You know, Frans Hals' flesh colors are also earthy, used here in the sense that you know. Often at least.

Sometimes, I almost dare say always, there is also a relation of contrast between the tone of the costume and the tone of the face....

Of [Jean-François] Millet, Rembrandt, and, for instance, Israels, it has truly been said that they are more harmonists than colorists.

But tell me, *black* and *white*, may they be used or may they not, are they forbidden fruit? I don't think so....

December 1885

Yesterday I saw a large photograph of a Rembrandt which I did not know, and which struck me tremendously; it was a woman's head, the light fell on the bust, neck, chin, and the tip of the nose—the lower jaw.

The forehead and eyes in the shadow of a large hat, with probably red feathers. Probably also red or yellow in the low-necked jacket. A dark background. The expression, a mysterious smile like that of Rembrandt himself in his self-portrait in which Saskia is sitting on his knee and he has a glass of wine in his hand [see p. 60].

These days my thoughts are full of Rembrandt and Hals all the time, not because I see so many of their pictures, but because among the people here I see so many types that remind me of that time.

I still go often to those popular balls, to see the heads of the women and the heads of the sailors and soldiers. One pays the entrance fee of 20 or 30 centimes, and drinks a glass of beer, for they drink very little spirits, and one can amuse oneself a whole evening, at least I do, by watching these people enjoy themselves. To paint a great deal from the model—that is what I must do, and it is the only thing that seriously helps to make progress....

I know that you are sufficiently convinced of the importance of being *true* so that I can speak out freely.

If I paint peasant women, I want them to be peasant women; for the same reason, if I paint harlots I want a harlot-like expression.

That was why a certain harlot's head by Rembrandt struck me so enormously. Because he had caught so infinitely beautifully that mysterious smile, with a gravity such as only he possesses, the magician of magicians.

This is a new thing for me, and it is essentially what I want.

May 1890

I am perhaps going to try to work from Rembrandt, I have especially an idea for doing the *Man at Prayer* in the scale of color from light yellow to violet.

Vincent van Gogh,
*The Complete Letters of
Vincent van Gogh,*
Translated by J. van Gogh-Bonger
and C. de Dood, 1958

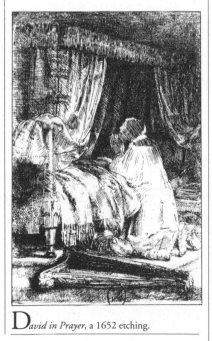

David in Prayer, a 1652 etching.

"It Is With Night That He Makes Day"

The French painter Eugène Fromentin was also an influential art critic. In The Masters of Past Time, *first published in 1876, he devoted several chapters to Rembrandt and* The Night Watch *(below).*

The Night Watch in the Trippenhuis

I shall surprise no one when I say that *The Night Watch* has no charm whatsoever, and this fact is without parallel among beautiful works of pictorial art. It astonishes and disconcerts, it obtrudes itself upon us, but it utterly lacks the primary insinuating attraction to win us over, and at first sight it nearly always displeases. First of all it offends that logic and habitual rectitude of the eye which likes distinct forms, lucid ideas, clearly formulated objectives; something warns you that the imagination, like the reason, will be only half-satisfied, and that the most easily persuaded of minds will succumb only in the long run, and will not yield

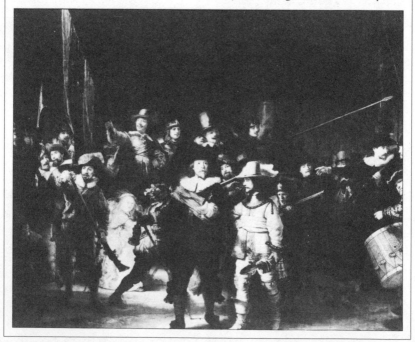

without argument. There are several reasons for this and not all are the fault of the picture—there is the light, which is detestable; the dark wooden frame, which makes the painting seem lost and fails to bring out either of its significant points, its bronze tone or its power, while causing it to look even more smoky than it really is; last and most important, there are the restrictions of space, which prevent the canvas being hung at a suitable height, and, contrary to all the most elementary laws of perspective, force you to view it close-up and on a level....

An Enigmatic Work?

You will be aware that *The Night Watch* is regarded, rightly or wrongly, as a virtually incomprehensible work, and this is one of the reasons for its great prestige. Perhaps it would have caused far less commotion in the world if, for the last two centuries, people had not continued the habit of looking for its meaning instead of examining its merits and persisted in the folly of viewing it as a picture which was above all else enigmatic.

Considering the work in its literal sense, what we know of the subject seems to me sufficient. First, we know the names and the occupations of the personages, for the painter carefully wrote them on a cartouche at the bottom of the picture; and this shows that, while the painter's fantasy has transfigured many things, the basic elements at any rate were taken from real life. We do not know the purpose for which these people are coming out with their weapons, whether they are going to shooting practice, on parade, or somewhere else; but as this is not a very profound mystery, I am sure that

if Rembrandt failed to be more explicit, it was because he did not want or did not know how to be more explicit, which paves the way to a whole series of hypothetical explanations ranging from want of ability to deliberate reticence.

As to the question about the time of day—the most disputed of all and also the only one that could have been settled at the outset—it really does not require an appreciation of the way the outstretched hand of the captain throws its shadow on the flap of a coat. It is enough to remember that Rembrandt always handled light in this way, that nocturnal darkness is habitual in his work, that shadow is his normal poetic idiom, his usual means of dramatic expression, and that in his portraits, in his interiors, in his rendering of legends and stories, in his landscapes, in his etchings, as in his paintings, it is with night that he makes day....

The Scene Is Indeterminate

It is generally acknowledged that the composition is not the principal merit of the work. The painter had not chosen the subject, and the way in which he set out to treat it did not leave scope for any great spontaneity or great lucidity in the initial realization. As a result, the scene is indeterminate, the action almost non-existent, and the focus of interest therefore very divided. An inherent defect in the basic idea, a sort of irresolution in the way it was conceived, arranged, and put into effect is apparent from the beginning. Some people walking, others coming to a halt, one priming his musket, another loading it, yet another firing, a drummer who shows his face as he beats his instrument, a somewhat theatrical standard-bearer, in short, a crowd of figures fixed in the immobility proper to portraits; and these, if I am not mistaken, are the only striking features of the picture when it comes to movement....

The Figures Are Out of Proportion

So there is no truth and little pictorial invention in the overall composition. Do the individual figures fare any better? I fail to see any which could be picked out as a choice piece of work.

What immediately strikes the eye is that there are disproportions between the figures without apparent reason, and in each case inadequacies and what one could call an anxiety to endow them with character which lacks any justification. The captain [the figure at the center front of the picture] is too tall and the lieutenant too short, not only when viewed next to Captain Cocq, whose size overwhelms him, but in relation to the auxiliary figures, whose height or breadth make this undersized young man look like a child with a premature moustache. Assessing them all as portraits, they can hardly be called successful, being dubious as likenesses, and unattractive as physiognomies, which is surprising in a portrait-painter who in 1642 had demonstrated his skill....

A Creature Half Woman, Half Firefly

There remains an episodic figure which has up till now baffled all conjecture, because it seems to personify in its traits, its dress, its strange brilliance, and its scant bearing on the subject, the magic, the romantic meaning, or, if you like, the alternative meaning of the picture. I mean the little person with the look of a witch, childish yet very old, with comet-like headdress and ornamented tresses, who glides, we scarcely understand why, among the legs of the guards, and who—a thing no less inexplicable—wears suspended from the waist a white cock, which could in a pinch be mistaken for a purse.

Whatever its reason for mixing with the assembly, this little figure seems to have nothing human about it at all. It is colorless, almost shapeless. Its age is uncertain because its traits are indefinable. Its appearance is that of a doll and its gait automatic. It has the mien of a beggar, and something like diamonds all over its body, the air of a little queen, with garments that look like rags.... She glimmers like pale fire, uncertain, flickering. The more closely one examines her, the less one can seize the subtle lines that somehow define her incorporeal existence. We come to see in her nothing but a form of remarkably strange phosphorescence which is not the natural light of reality, nor yet the ordinary brilliancy of a well-calculated artist's palette, and which adds one more element of witchery to the strangeness of the physiognomy. Note that in the place she occupies in one of the dark corners of the canvas, rather low, in the middle distance, between a man in dark red and the captain dressed in black, this eccentric light is all the more effective for the fact it is in startling contrast to its surroundings; and that, without careful safeguards, this explosion of accidental light could of itself have disorganized the whole picture....

Rembrandt the Colorist

The only points on which opinion is unanimous, particularly nowadays, are the coloring of the picture, which is

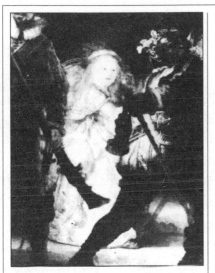

At her waist this mysterious small female figure bears various symbols of archery.

There Is No Abstract Light

Does Rembrandt work in this way? You have only to look at *The Night Watch* to observe the contrary.

Apart from one or two bold colors, two reds and a dark violet, apart from one or two sparks of blue, you can see nothing in this colorless and violent canvas which resembles the palette and the ordinary method of any of the established colorists. The heads have the semblance rather than the coloring of life. They are red, vinous, or pale, yet they do not have the realistic pallor that Velázquez gives his faces, nor the sanguine, yellowish, greyish, or purple shades that Frans Hals so delicately sets against each other when he wants to portray the temperaments of his figures. In the clothes, the headdresses, the very various items of apparel, the color is no more accurate or expressive than is, as I have said, the form itself. When a red is featured, it is not a very subtle red and it depicts silk, cloth, or satin indiscriminately. The guardsman loading his musket is dressed in red from head to foot, from his felt hat to his shoes. Do you perceive that the physiognomic peculiarities of this red, its nature and substance, which a true colorist would never have failed to seize, has only for a moment engaged Rembrandt's attention? This red is said to be admirably logical in its light and in its shade. In truth, I don't think that anyone, however unpracticed in manipulating tonal qualities, could hold such an opinion—and I don't suppose that either Velázquez or Veronese, Titian, or Giorgione, to say nothing of Rubens, would have accepted the way it is composed and laid on. I challenge anyone to tell me

described as "dazzling," "blinding," "unheard-of" (you will agree that words of this nature seem calculated to make one disregard them), and the execution, which is generally agreed to be masterly. The question becomes very delicate....

Reduced to the simplest of terms, the issue is as follows: to choose colors beautiful in themselves, and secondarily, to combine them in beautiful, skillful, and exact relationship. I will add that the colors may be deep or light, of rich tint or neutral, in other words duller; "bold," in other words nearer the *original color* of the objects; or graded and "broken," to use a technical term, and lastly, of diverse value (I have told you elsewhere what is meant by that)—all this is a matter of temperament, of preference, and also of suitability....

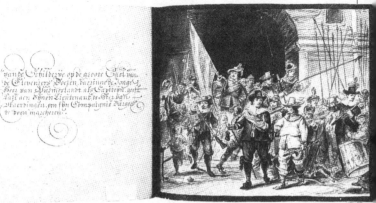

T his watercolor copy of *The Night Watch* made in 1650 in Captain Cocq's album shows the painting before it was cut down.

---

how the lieutenant is dressed, or the color of his costume. Is it white tinted with yellow? Is it a yellow so pale as to seem almost white? The truth is that as this person had to convey the central light of the picture, Rembrandt clothed him in light—very skillfully in terms of brilliance, very carelessly in terms of color.

Now, and this is where Rembrandt begins to betray himself as a colorist, there is no abstract light. Light in itself is nothing: It is the product of colors variously illumined and variously radiating, according to the nature of the ray that they reflect or absorb. One very dark tint may be extraordinarily luminous; another very light one may on the other hand not be so at all. Every student knows that. To colorists, then, light depends exclusively on the choice of colors used to render it and is so closely bound up with the tone that we can truly say that for them light and color are one. In *The Night Watch* there is nothing like this. The tone disappears

in the light, just as it disappears in the shade. The shade is blackish, the light whitish. Everything is brightened or darkened, everything radiates or is obscured by an oscillating effacement of the coloring principle....

Chiaroscuro

I come at last to the undeniable interest of the picture, to Rembrandt's great impetus in a new direction: I am referring to the application on a grand scale of his own particular way of seeing, which has been called chiaroscuro....

No one used it so continuously and ingeniously. It is the mysterious form *par excellence*, the most shrouded, the most elliptical, the most suggestive, the most capable of surprise to exist in the pictorial vocabulary of artists. For this reason it is, above all others, the medium of intimate feelings and ideas. It is light, vaporous, veiled, discreet; it lends its charm to elusive things, incites curiosity, adds grace to intellectual speculation. It partakes of feelings, emotions, uncertainty, the indefinite and the infinite, dreams and the ideal. And this is why it is, why it had to be, the natural poetic framework in which Rembrandt's genius constantly operated. Rembrandt's work, then, in all its inwardness and truth, can fittingly be studied in this, the usual form of his thought. And if, instead of skimming over the surface, I were to plumb the depths of this vast subject, you would see his whole psychological being materialize from the mists of the chiaroscuro; however, I shall say only what I need to say, and Rembrandt will emerge no less clearly, I hope....

The consequences of this way of seeing, feeling, and rendering the elements of actual life are easily imagined. The world has a changed appearance. Defining lines are attenuated or effaced, colors are volatilized. The modeling, no longer confined by a rigid contour, becomes less definite in its stroke, more undulating in its surfaces, and when carried out by a practiced and sensitive hand it is at its most lifelike and convincing, for it holds a thousand artifices which give it what one could call a double life—one that springs from nature and another that has its source in the conveying of emotion. In summary, there are ways of giving a canvas depth and distance, of bringing it close, of dissimulating, of rendering apparent, and of burying the true in the imaginary: this is *art*, or more precisely, *the art of chiaroscuro.*

The Light of Visions

Rembrandt's whole career, then, is shaped by a constant objective: to paint only with the aid of light, to draw only with light. And all the varied criticisms

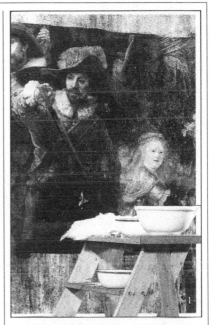

The *Night Watch* (detail) in 1975, during the restoration that removed the "night."

that have been made of his works, beautiful or flawed, doubtful or incontestable, may be turned into one simple question: Should he or should he not have attached so exclusive an importance to light? Did the subject demand it, admit of it, or exclude it? If the first, it grows out of the spirit of the work; it cannot help but be admirable. If the second, the outcome is uncertain, and the work is nearly always questionable or ill conceived....

In terms of the painter's tendency to portray a subject only by the lightness and darkness of things, *The Night Watch* holds...no further secrets.

Eugène Fromentin
The Masters of Past Time, 1876

Writers on Rembrandt

Rembrandt has inspired poetic reflection as have few painters before or since. The ambiguity and power of his work strike a chord with partisans of both the sacred and the profane —different expressions of the same disquiet.

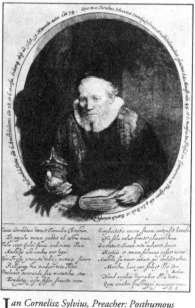

J an Cornelisz Sylvius, Preacher: Posthumous Portrait, a 1646 etching.

Paul Claudel: The Sacrament of Light

It was a milestone in the history of art when painting ceased to have a ceremonial or decorative role and began, in complete freedom, simply to look at reality and build up a repertoire of signs and symbols whose lines and colors could be combined to yield a meaning. The Dutch artist was no longer a will that carried out a preconceived plan to which method and movement were subordinated, he was an eye that selected and grasped, he was a mirror that painted; everything he did followed from a *reflection*, from an expert exposure of the plate to the lens; all the figures that he gave us seemed to have come back from a voyage to the land of the looking glass. The gradation of shadows, the administration of a scale of values around the focal center, the dilution or precision of detail, corresponding to the intensity and concentration of attention, the spot of luminosity that shapes the whole in relation to itself and strangely gives rise to all kinds of scintillating effects, gradations, reflections, and echoes, the importance given to emptiness and to space itself, all the silence released by an object that ensnares the eye, all this, was not invented or practiced by Rembrandt alone. He was not the first nor the only one who knew how to give a canvas soul by lighting it, if I may put it thus, from behind and who knew how to marry light to the gaze, a gaze that gave being to a face by illuminating it. But where others tested a process hesitantly, he applied it with the wholeheartedness and authority of a master. All those portraits around us are not records of human life studied and elaborated with the application of a historian or a moralist. Those men, those women, have made acquaintance with the night; they come back to us not so much repulsed as stopped by a thicker medium. Bathed in a light taken from memory, they have reached self-awareness. They come forward and stir an echo there where in the artist's heart and in the deepest entrails of the earth the forces of creation and reproduction lie dormant. Along the route to extinction they have made a U-turn. They have achieved a permanence that our frail mind gropingly tries to realize. Stamped with personality, they give new life to the effigy by isolating it… worked by circumstance and character, which lay buried in the everyday.

Hence comes the special atmosphere emitted by Rembrandt's pictures and etchings, the sense of dream, of something somnolent, confined, and taciturn, a sort of corruption of the night, a sort of mental acidity at grips with the shadows which under our eyes indefinitely continues its corroding activity. The art of the great Dutchman is no longer a hearty affirmation of the here and now, a burst of the imagination in the realm of the actual, a feast for our senses, the perpetuation of a moment of joy and color. It is no longer a present on which to gaze, it is an invitation to remember. One has the impression that the painter goes with each of his models' gestures, each of their attitudes, each of their interactions with the group, in his retrospective voyage beyond the surface and the here and now, a voyage which is indefinitely prolonged and which reaches its end less in the outlines than in the reverberations. The stimulus has stirred recollection, and recollection, surfacing

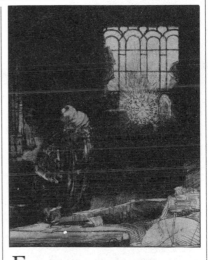

*F*aust in His Study, a 1652 etching.

in its turn, successively disturbs the superimposed layers of memory, summons other related images….

But never in front of a picture by Rembrandt does one have a sense of the permanent and definitive: It is a precarious creation, a phenomenon, a miraculous return to the past— the curtain raised for an instant is poised to fall back, the reflection fades away, the light in shifting by a margin extinguishes the marvel, the visitor who a moment ago was there has disappeared, we hardly had the time to recognize him *in the instant of breaking bread*, or, if he is still there, by this special insistence, in this magic apparition, one could say rather that he lives on. There is something here comparable to the phenomenon of the tide of which I spoke earlier, to that alternative life that animates Holland, to a fullness so total one feels that on all sides it is already preparing for the ebb. But in Rembrandt it is not a matter of water swelling our tissues and penetrating our substance. It is a matter of light, which for him is like sap, which both sustains thought and emanates from it. How he loved light! How he understood its play and its purposes, the screens which open and close on all sides of the sky, the special slant of the sunbeam that visits, crosses, investigates our inner dwelling and our powers of thought! The Egyptians and the Greeks in a world of enduring stone and intellectual thought raised naked, flowing forms, a conversation of gods remote and sacred. Rembrandt, however, is the master of the ray of light, of the gaze and all that comes to life and speech beneath the gaze, which illuminates less than it coaxes figures and objects to a corresponding life....

We have covered the prodigious gallery at a pace both hesitant and rapid and now we have arrived in the central hall, which is solely occupied and filled by the huge exhibit known as *The Night Watch*. It is this, across Holland and in the middle of Amsterdam, in the middle of all the painting of the Golden Age, which is touched by its glory, that I had promised myself, a good while ago, after reading the tantalizing book by Fromentin, to visit.

Immediately, as soon as one reopens one's eyes, as soon as one recovers from the soft shock of this gold amassed and distilled in the deepest reaches of the spirit, of this light that is like a purified and concentrated element, like visible thought, of this form of psychological blow, what strikes one is the composition. The two principal figures, one the Dominator, in black with a red sash and the other—the other, how to describe his attire?—who trail behind them the rest of the group, but their feet are actually on the edge of the frame! One step more—one sees that the veteran's gesture is urging his luminous companion to take it—and from the dark gateway in the rear through which they emerged they would pass into the realm of the invisible. But what about all those other people standing by behind them, it is not for nothing they have armed themselves, brandishing all those strange weapons, will they not also start to advance? Yes indeed! From front to rear the painter has laid down all the gradations and all the nuances of movement getting under way, we even feel ourselves imitating the posture the first

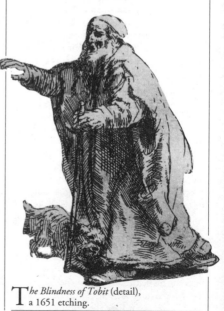

The Blindness of Tobit (detail), a 1651 etching.

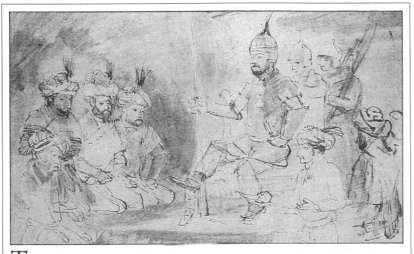

The Emperor Timur on the Throne (c. 1635), a drawing after an Indian miniature.

leg assumes when the other is already bending in readiness to advance! The flag is unfurled, the drum rolls or, rather, is about to roll. It even seems to me that I hear the report of a gun.

Paul Claudel
Dutch Painting, 1935

Display, Decrepitude, and Goodness

A great goodness. And I use this word to move quickly. His last portrait seems to say this: "My intelligence is such that even wild animals will recognize my goodness." The moral sense that drove him was not a vain quest for spiritual improvement—it was exacted by his work, or, rather, bound up with it. We know this because, by a chance almost unique in the history of art, a painter who posed in front of the mirror with an almost narcissistic readiness has left us, in parallel with his work, a series of self-portraits in which we can read the evolution of his method and the action

of this evolution on the man. Or is it the other way around?

In the pictures he painted before 1642 Rembrandt appeared enamored of display, but a display that went no further than the scene represented. The sumptuousness—in Oriental portraits, biblical scenes—lay in the richness of the decors, the accessories; Jeremiah wears a very pretty robe, he rests his foot on a rich carpet, the vases on the rock are of gold, it is visible. One senses Rembrandt happy to invent or portray a conventional richness, and likewise happy to paint the extravagant *Saskia as Flora* [see pp. 58 and 142], or himself with Saskia on his knees, magnificently dressed, raising his glass [see p. 60]. He had of course from his youth painted those of lowly status—often decking them out in glorious rags—and it seemed that while he dreamed of splendor he at the same time had a predilection for the faces of the humble. With rare exceptions the sensuality that touched his brush when he painted a textile, for example, retreated when he approached a face. Even in his youth he preferred faces ravaged by age....

It has been written: Rembrandt, unlike, for example, Hals, was not skilled at getting a likeness in his portraits—in other words, at seeing the difference between one man and

This etching of a *Beggar Seated on a Bank* (detail), 1630, is a self-portrait.

another. If he did not see it, was it perhaps because it did not exist? His portraits in fact rarely convey a trait of the sitter's character. The man who is there is not, *a priori*, either weak, or cowardly, or tall, or short, or good, or wicked. He is capable, at any point, of being these things. But never is the character trait apparently preordained....

Except for Titus—who was his son— smiling, not one of his faces is serene. All seem burdened by a drama, laden. The figures, nearly always, in their grouped and concentrated attitudes, suggest a tornado in a moment's respite. They carry a weighty destiny, which they precisely evaluate, and which from one moment to the next they will pursue to its end. While Rembrandt's own drama seems to be no other than his observation of the world. He wants to know what it is all about, in order to free himself. All his figures carry the knowledge of a wound, and seek refuge from it. Rembrandt knows he is wounded, but he wants to be cured. Hence the impression of vulnerability when we look at his self-portraits, and the impression of confident strength when we are before his other pictures....

Rembrandt? Excepting a few swashbuckling portraits, all, from his earliest youth, reveal a troubled spirit in pursuit of a truth that evades him. The sharpness of his eye is not wholly explained by a compulsion to stare hard at the mirror. At times he even has an air almost wicked (remember that he actually paid to have a creditor put in prison!), vain (the arrogance of the ostrich plume on the velvet hat...and the golden neckaces...), but, little by little, the hardness of the countenance softened. In front of the mirror narcissistic satisfaction turned to anxiety and an impassioned, then tremulous, quest.

For some time he lived with Hendrickje, and this marvelous woman...must have satisfied both his sensuality and his need for tenderness. In his last self-portraits one no longer reads psychological signs. If one cares to, one can see there the advent of something like an air of goodness. Or detachment? Whatever one wishes. Here it comes to the same thing.

Toward the end of his life Rembrandt became good. So the mask or defense was withdrawn, the screen against the world presented by wickedness. Wickedness, and all forms of aggression, and all that we call traits of character, our humors, our desires, eroticism, and vanities. Shatter the screen then to bring the world closer! But this goodness—or if one prefers detachment—was not something he had sought in order to obey a moral or religious rule (it is only, if ever, in an artist's moments of abandon that he can have faith) or to acquire a few virtues. If he had tested in the flames what one can term his characteristics, it was to have a purer vision of the world and make a truer work with it. I imagine that he ultimately did not care whether he was good or wicked, bad-tempered or patient, grasping or generous.... His task was to be but an eye and a hand. In addition, following this same egoistic path, he had to earn —what a word—the kind of purity so manifest in his last portrait as to be almost wounding. But it was clearly by painting that he attained it....

Around the years 1666 to 1669 there must have been in Amsterdam something other than the paintings of an old crook (if the story of the repossessed etching plates is true) and the city. There was what remained of a person reduced to extremity, almost completely extinguished, going from bed to easel, from easel to lavatory— where he continued to do rough sketches with his dirty fingernails—and what remained was scarcely more than a cruel goodness, not far removed from imbecility. A furrowed hand that held brushes soaked in red and brown, an eye resting on objects, nothing but this, and the intelligence that linked the eye to the world was without hope.

In his last self-portrait he is quietly having a laugh. Quietly. He knows everything a painter can learn. And most of all this (well, perhaps?), that the painter is wholly concentrated in the eye that goes from the object to the canvas, and above all in the gesture of the hand that goes from the little pool of color to the canvas.

The painter is concentrated there, in the sure and tranquil movement of the hand. Nothing but this in the world: the tranquil and trembling to and fro into which all the display, the sumptuousness, the obsessions have been transmuted. Legally there is nothing else. Thanks to a trick of signatures, everything is in the hands of Hendrickje the Admirable and Titus. Rembrandt does not even own the canvases on which he paints.

A man has just gone by wholly taken up by his work. What else is left of him is good for the garbage dump, but before, just before, he must again paint *The Return of the Prodigal Son.*

He died before he was tempted to play the buffoon.

Jean Genet
The Secret of Rembrandt, 1958

Art Historians and Rembrandt

Holland, chiaroscuro, history, religion, and mythology all raise questions for the art historian studying Rembrandt. His legendary and mysterious personality precludes a single or definitive answer.

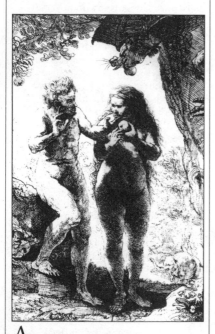

A*dam and Eve* (detail), 1638.

"He Handled the World Like an Unceasing Drama"

Every Dutchman is born a painter at heart, and he cannot be otherwise. For this native gift to develop in a few minds, and be put into practice, it requires only that a moment of enthusiasm, a brief spurt of exertion set a generation or two in motion. There is not a country in the world where history and the terrain have more directly influenced the artist's rendering of life. And, whatever may have been said, Rembrandt is no exception.

However, this needs to be explained. What the thousand painters of Holland take as the subject of their canvases, Rembrandt uses as the raw material of his visions. Where the others see facts, he perceives hidden connections that link his preternatural sensibility to reality and transport all that he has religiously drawn from the universal creation to the plane of a new creation.

And as those among whom he lives feel only indifference to him, as his strange vision passes over the heads of the mass, he appears to be outside the mass, and even in a state of permanent antagonism to it.

And yet he speaks its language, it is of it that he speaks to us, and thence of he who finds there the roots of his suffering, and of his understanding, and love and hate, before mastering emotion and passion, the better to accept it as a living destiny and merge it within himself to other images of the world which he elevated together to the impartial force of his own mind.

Where then would Rembrandt have

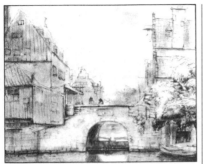

View of the Bridge at Grimnesse-sluis in Amsterdam, now attributed to Rembrandt's pupil Abraham Furnerius.

found his gold and his reds, and the silvery or reddish light where sun and spray mingle, had he not ever lived in Amsterdam, in the corner of the city that was most teeming, most squalid, near the boats unloading red rags on to the quay, rusted scrap iron, smoked herring, gingerbread, and a sumptuous trail of scarlets and yellows on the day of the flower market?

Through the ferment of the dirty streets of the Jewish quarter, where colored cloths hung at the windows, brightening the russet shadows with a fiery glow, he made his way, along the lanes of water which lapped and reflected the ornamented facades, the painted cloths, as far as the banks of the Amstel, where, in the brilliant evenings of seaside cities, the great ships unloaded embroidered textiles, tropical fruits, exotic birds.

Where then would he have acquired his taste for imaginary voyages, for glimpses of distant seas, for the magic Orient that he saw as dust dancing in a ray of sun, when it sent its beams to the depths of the cellars where dampness seeped in from the canals?

And when he entered the hovels where the usurers of the ghetto weighed gold on a balance, where poor families were huddled, dressed in singed tatters, in makeshift calico rags, where in the darkness junk dealers piled iron breastplates, inlaid weapons, worked copper and leather, how could he have failed to stumble on scenes that no one attends to as soon as poverty is the norm, mothers baring their breasts to suckle their children, the old dying on straw mattresses, sores wrapped in dirty cloth, and the rediscovered innocence of hunger and love?…

The same driving force operates choice, takes the world as an inexhaustible repository of movable symbols to be employed at will, but the will can only learn to use them as it requires, when it has understood the internal forces of which space and the masses that occupy it are the manifestation.…

That which is immersed in light is the reverberation of that which is plunged in night. That which is plunged in night extends into the invisible that which is immersed in light. Thought, gaze, word, action connect this brow, this eye, this mouth, this hand on the books, hardly noticed in the shadow, heads and bodies bent around a birth, an agony, or a death.

Even, and perhaps above all, when his working tools were only his steel point, his copperplate, his acid, nothing but black and white, even then he handled the world like an unceasing drama that day and darkness shaped, carved, convulsed, calmed, and made live and die according to his desire, his sadness, the desperate longing for eternity, and the absolute that gripped his heart.

Elie Faure
History of Art, Modern Art
Vol. 4, 1921–7

Rembrandt: "The Least Classical and the Most Romantic of All Painters"

If ever there was a man of genius in art, it was Rembrandt. He might be said to have created a medium of his own, through which he saw all objects. He was the grossest and the least vulgar, that is to say the least commonplace in his grossness, of all men. He was the most downright, the least fastidious of the imitators of nature. He took any object, he cared not what, how

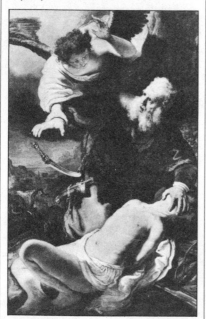

A *braham's Sacrifice* (1636).

mean soever in form, colour, and expression, and from the light and shade which he threw upon it, it came out gorgeous from his hands.

As van Dyck made one of the smallest contrasts of light and shade, and painted as if in the open air, Rembrandt used the most violent and abrupt contrasts in this respect, and painted his objects as if in a dungeon. His pictures may be said to be "bright with excessive darkness." His vision had acquired a lynx-eyed sharpness from the artificial obscurity to which he had accustomed himself. "Mystery and silence hung upon his pencil."

Yet he could pass rapidly from one extreme to another, and dip his colours with equal success in the gloom of night, or in the blaze of the noonday sun. In surrounding different objects with a medium of imagination, solemn or dazzling, he was a true poet; in all the rest he was a mere painter, but a painter of no common stamp.

The powers of his hand were equal to those of his eye; and indeed he could not have attempted the subjects he did, without an execution as masterly as his knowledge was profound. His colours are sometimes dropped in lumps on the canvas; at other times they are laid on as smooth as glass, and he not unfrequently painted with the handle of his brush....

His history and landscapes are equally fine in their way. His landscapes we could look at forever, though there is nothing in them.... It seems as if he had dug them out of nature.

Every thing is so true, so real, so full of all the feelings and associations which the eye can suggest to the other senses, that we immediately take as strong an affection to them as if they were our home—the very place where we were brought up. No length of time could add to the intensity of the impression they convey. Rembrandt is the least classical and the most romantic of all painters.

William Hazlitt
"Fine Arts," *Encyclopaedia Britannica*
1817

A Fundamental Part of Rembrandt's Character: His "Angry Impatience With Convention"

It is sometimes said that the character of Rembrandt as the rebel artist is an invention of romanticism; and it is true that during the 19th century the Rembrandt legend, especially the story of his fall from popularity and social ostracism, was given more dramatic coloring. But that the young man from Leiden saw himself as a tough and rebellious character is made perfectly clear to us in a whole series of self-portraits.

The earliest of these [right], a drawing in the British Museum, is the very image of a rebel, with thick lips and strawberry nose; and the earliest etching [see p. 102 center], done about a year later, is scarcely more refined, the truculent expression being rendered by an equally bold and truculent line.

Most conclusive of all is the etching [see p. 154] where he has portrayed himself as one of his favorite beggars snarling at the prosperous, bourgeois society which was shortly to welcome him so warmly. This angry impatience with convention was a fundamental part of Rembrandt's character, and although he managed to control it during his years of prosperity, it came out strongly in his middle life and is emphasized in the three early

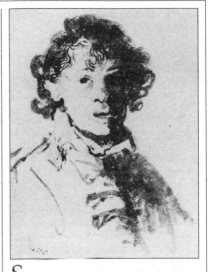

Self Portrait (c. 1627–8).

biographies written by men who had first-hand information about him.

Kenneth Clark
Rembrandt and the Italian Renaissance
1966

Science and Art: The Rembrandt Research Project

Questions of authenticity have frequently arisen about Rembrandt's work. At the beginning of the 20th century the catalogue of his creations listed over one thousand pictures. Today, as a result of much study, the total is approximately one quarter of that.

How many will the catalogue include when the scholars of the Rembrandt Research Project have completed their investigations? The process will take many more years and even then we will not be sure: Their results are disputed by some experts.

Here, the team explains its history, objectives, and methods.

Is there any need for a new catalogue of Rembrandt's paintings? It was the growing conviction that such is the case that led to the Rembrandt Research Project. There is, of course, a wealth of scholarly literature on the subject, but it is hard to avoid the impression that much of its interpretation of the artist and his work is based on a picture of his painted oeuvre that in the course of time has become corrupted. By the 1960s it was difficult for an impartial eye to accept all the works currently attributed to Rembrandt as being by a single artist....

Research naturally began from the point which studies of Rembrandt had reached in the 1960s, though without explicitly analyzing the situation as it then was.

As time went on, however, we became confirmed in our impression that there is scarcely any verifiable, documented continuity in respect to the attribution of Rembrandt's paintings such as there has been, to some extent, for his etchings from the 17th century onward. Such continuity does exist for a tiny handful of paintings, but it is hard to describe these as a representative nucleus; they leave the limits of the painted oeuvre entirely undefined....

[Already at the end of the 19th century] knowledge of the work done by pupils grew, and undoubtedly this helped to bring about a sharper picture of Rembrandt's own production. Yet only clearly identifiable works by these pupils were involved in this process of separation; what remained formed a remarkably heterogeneous and extensive oeuvre....

To [Horst] Gerson, whose publications appeared when our project was in its initial stage (1968 and 1969), goes the honor of having had the courage to bring open-mindedness to his critical approach to the received image....

Given the possibility of maintaining contact with experts in other fields whenever necessary, we decided that the homogeneity of method and results would be served best by forming a team consisting of art historians only....

A second basic principle was to try to learn and describe the features—including the purely physical features—of each painting seen as an object, as fully as possible....

For the bulk of the paintings, however, examination had to be limited to what could be seen at the surface, and the interpretation of what was observed must, however usable this might be for comparative purposes, be termed an overall one. We have, for example, called the layer that shows through discontinuities or translucent patches in the paint layer simply "the ground" without further distinction, and have referred to it as such in our descriptions. It was only at a late stage that we formed the hypothesis that this layer (usually a light, yellowish brown) is in some cases not the actual ground but rather part of the preparatory brush drawing on top of it, executed in predominantly translucent brown; while the ground proper does show through this, it is not necessarily directly visible....

The most familiar technique, and one which the art historian has known for a long time, is the X-ray photograph…. For us, the importance of X-rays came to lie mainly in understanding how the young Rembrandt set out his composition, applied the first layer of paint, and worked toward completion….

Dendrochronology [a method of dating based on the annual growth rings of trees] has opened up new perspectives for the dating of oak panels [underneath the paint]….

Physical and chemical examination of sample material from the ground and paint layers already occupies a fairly important role in the literature, but this is only seldom clearly related to what the art historian is seeking….

Without being unfair to either, we might perhaps say that the scientist arrives at his interpretation from relatively fragmentary and, of itself, unstructured information relating to the physical make-up of the work of art, while the art historian is concerned mainly with the stylistic interpretation of the picture and its execution….

In general, we have limited ourselves, in most catalogue entries, to dealing with present knowledge in iconography and, in a few cases, to making suggestions based on views gained from this. Sometimes these differ sharply from commonly held and still rather romantically tinged ideas of the meaning that Rembrandt's pictures may have held for him and his contemporaries.

Some Reflections on Method

We realized…that the results of scientific examination would never be able to provide proof of whether a painting was by Rembrandt himself, by

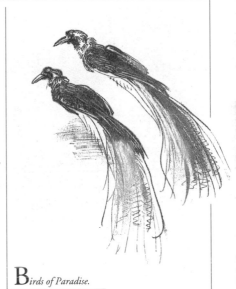

Birds of Paradise.

one of his pupils, or by a painter in his immediate circle. We did hope for firm evidence in the category of works that we believed, on stylistic grounds, might be later imitations of Rembrandt's style…. We found not only that the number of "demonstrably later" paintings was almost negligible, but even that some of those that we had, because of stylistic features, regarded as being 18th or 19th century in origin could be proved, or virtually proved, to date from the 17th….

In our catalogue entries the reader will find no poetry. We positively mistrust poetic evocations of Rembrandtish qualities. Deeply felt songs of praise have been written in the past about highly suspect paintings in which no one believes today. The tone in our catalogue is usually very down-to-earth.

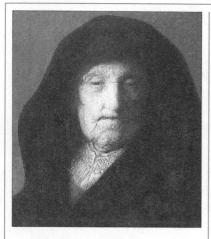 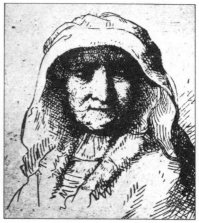

The Rembrandt Research Project team divides the works it has examined into three categories:

A = a genuine Rembrandt,
B = a work questionably by Rembrandt,
C = a work wrongly attributed to Rembrandt.

Example of a Work Not Accepted as by Rembrandt: C. 42, *Bust of an Old Woman* (commonly called *Rembrandt's Mother*)

Summarized opinion
An imitation [above left], based on the etching B. 353 [above right], which was formerly wrongly attributed to Rembrandt....

Comments
The extremely disorganized handling of paint, with strange color accents (in the lit eyelid and elsewhere), together with the superabundance of scratchmarks that frequently fail to show form as they are intended to do, make it impossible to believe that the painting was done by Rembrandt or even within his circle. The execution is so coarse, and there is so little suggestion of form, that it must rather be described as an extremely superficial attempt to achieve a Rembrandt-like effect. One can comment, furthermore, that neither the flat, opaque gray background nor the use of so much flat, thin gray-black devoid of modeling is imaginable in Rembrandt or his pupils....

This conclusion can be supported with two arguments. In the first place, the old woman has been painted on top of another picture which, so far as one can see from the X-ray, is laid in with a most unusual technique that must be termed inconceivable for a 17th-century Dutch painting. This first, apparently uncompleted painting was still not fully dry when the present picture was done on top of it; this can be assumed from the fissure-like nature of the irregular craquelure.

In the second place, the portrait does not, as has been generally assumed

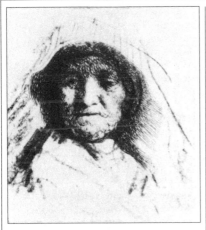

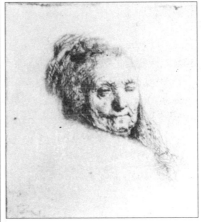

in the literature, resemble Rembrandt's etching B. 352 [above left] of an old woman, of 1628, but rather etching B. 353 [opposite right]. This latter etching has long been regarded as an imitation of B. 352 in combination with B. 354; it was attributed by A. D. de Vries Az. (in: O.H. 1, 1883, p. 294) to Samuel van Hoogstraten and by C. White and K. G. Boon (Hollst. XVIII, p. 183, no. B. 353) to Michael Lukas Leopold Willmann (Königsberg 1630—Kloster Leubus 1706). This etching was clearly the prototype for the painting, which with one or two variations (the cast shadow of the head-shawl does not extend so far downward) resembles it so closely that the apparently arbitrary scratchmarks on the cheek at the left and elsewhere become understandable as borrowed from the etching.

The date of no. C. 42 cannot for the moment be determined with any accuracy. Etching B. 353 provides a *terminus post quem* of shortly after 1650. Closer investigation of the type

Which of these portraits is a fake? The Rembrandt Research Project questions the authenticity of the two on p. 162.

of wood used for the panel and, if possible, dendrochronological measurements might perhaps yield more precise information.

Summary

From the execution—in itself confused, and differing in brushwork and use of color from the habits of Rembrandt and his school—from the interpretation of the underlying painting seen in the X-ray, and from the use made, as a prototype, of an etching once wrongly attributed to Rembrandt, one must conclude that no. C. 42 is an imitation. There is every reason to assume that it was not done until the second half of the 17th century at the earliest.

Selected passages from Rembrandt Research Project, *A Corpus of Rembrandt Paintings*, Vol. 1, 1982

Picture This

Rembrandt, in his self-portraits, was his own best biographer. Others have sought to link his various figures to his life. Joseph Heller made Rembrandt a character in a novel, which allowed him to invent the answer to the puzzle.

Rembrandt painting Aristotle contemplating the bust of Homer was himself contemplating the bust of Homer where it stood on the red cloth covering the square table in the left foreground and wondering how much money it might fetch at the public auction of his belongings that he was already contemplating was sooner or later going to be more or less inevitable.

Aristotle could have told him it would not fetch much. The bust of Homer was a copy.

It was an authentic Hellenistic imitation of a Hellenic reproduction of a statue for which there had never been an authentic original subject....

About the money to be paid for the painting there could be no doubt. The terms had been set beforehand in correspondence between the Sicilian nobleman ordering the work and Dutch agents in Amsterdam, one of whom, probably, should be credited with proposing Rembrandt for the commission and bringing together these two figures significant in the art world of the 17th century who would never meet, whose association as patron and performer spanned more than eleven years, and between whom there would pass at least one acrimonious exchange of messages in which the purchaser complained he was cheated and the artist responded he was not.... The price of the painting was five hundred guilders.

Five hundred guilders was a good piece of money in the Netherlands back in 1653, even in Amsterdam, where the cost of living tended to be higher than elsewhere in the province of Holland and in the six other provinces making up the newly recognized and rather loosely organized federation of the United Netherlands, or the Dutch Republic.

Five hundred guilders was eight times the amount, Don Antonio Ruffo complained angrily in writing nine years later, that he would have had to pay to an Italian artist for a picture the size he had commissioned. He did not know that it was perhaps *ten* times the amount Rembrandt could then have demanded in Amsterdam, where he was past the peak of his fashionability and facing a financial catastrophe whose drastic consequences were to keep him impoverished for the rest of his life....

In 1961, the cost of the painting to the Metropolitan Museum of Art was a record $2,300,000.

For five hundred guilders in Amsterdam in 1653, a busy artisan or shopkeeper could support himself and his family rather well for a full year. A house in the city could be bought for that much....

For the widower Rembrandt van Rijn, who had bought his house for thirteen thousand guilders and who had lived *very* well in the ten or eleven years in which his reputation had dimmed

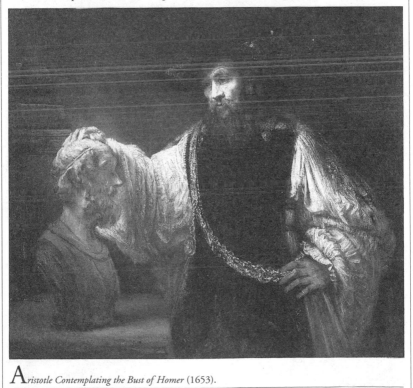

A*ristotle Contemplating the Bust of Homer* (1653).

and the income he had grown used to had lessened, five hundred guilders was not going to be enough.

After fourteen years, he still owed more than nine thousand guilders on his house, an obligation he was to have satisfied in six. The country was at war with England, her occasional Protestant ally in her long revolution against Spain. And this time it was already clear that the Dutch were not going to win. There was plague in the city. Financial discouragement was epidemic. The economy was poor, capital was growing scarce, and the owners of the debt were insisting they be paid.

Rembrandt's house was a luxurious urban mansion of the Dutch kind in a choice residential area on one of the broadest and most fashionable avenues in the east side of the city, the St. Anthoniesbreestraat. The word *bree-straat*, by which the excellent thorough-fare was known in its diminutive, translates literally into "broad street."

It was next to a corner site amid other dwellings of similar restrained elegance in which resided a number of the city's wealthiest burghers and officials, several of whom had been his first patrons and sponsors. When Rembrandt bought it, the initial expenses had been met with money from the dowry of his wife, Saskia, combined with his own considerable earnings in the years he was extolled in Amsterdam and his career as a painter was flourishing.

Between 1632 and 1633, it is reported, young Rembrandt executed fifty paintings in a deluge of commissions he received after moving from Leiden to Amsterdam in 1631, when he was twenty-five. Fifty in two years averages out to just about one painting every two weeks.

If the figure is a lie, it is a very impressive lie, and there is no doubt that Rembrandt and Saskia, who was the orphaned daughter of a former burgomaster of Leeuwarden in Friesland, and the cousin of his esteemed art dealer in Amsterdam, had considerable social legitimacy with the city's middle class. In Holland in the 17th century, the middle class was the upper class.

Now, Rembrandt had debts that he could not meet.

Rembrandt contemplated often as he worked on Aristotle contemplating the bust of Homer that he was going to have to either sell the house or borrow from friends to finish paying for it, and he knew that he was going to borrow.

As he added more and more black to Aristotle's robe and put still more

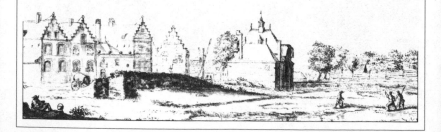

mixtures of black into a background of innumerable dark shadings—he enjoyed watching the way his canvases drank up black—he contemplated also that after he had borrowed from friends to finish paying for the house, he would put the house in the name of his small son, Titus, to protect it from seizure by these friends when he decided not to repay them.

He could not take more money from the legacy of Titus, who was too young to know that his father had taken any money from him at all.

Rembrandt was forty-seven, and facing ruin.

Saskia had died eleven years earlier. Of the four children born to Mr. and Mrs. Rembrandt van Rijn in the eight years of their marriage, Titus, the last of the four, was the only one to live longer than two months.

Aristotle contemplating Rembrandt contemplating Aristotle often imagined, when Rembrandt's face fell into a moody look of downcast introspection, similar in feeling and somber hue to the one Rembrandt was painting on him, that Rembrandt contemplating Aristotle contemplating the bust of Homer might also be contemplating in lamentation his years with Saskia. The death of a happy marriage, Aristotle knew from experience, is no small thing, nor is the death of three children.

Rembrandt lived now with a woman named Hendrickje Stoffels, who had come into his house as a maidservant and soon would be carrying his child.

Aristotle could understand that too....

Aristotle, so thorough and correct in drawing his own will, had to wonder occasionally what went on in the mind of the notary who had assisted Saskia

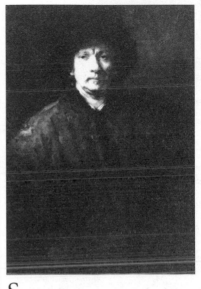

Self-Portrait (1652).

van [Ulenborch] with hers....

"Why do all your people look so sad now?" inquired the tall man modeling for Aristotle.

"They worry."

"What do they worry about?"

"Money," said the artist.

But that kind of tremulous solemnity was absent from his own face in the domineering self-portrait of 1652 [above] on the opposite side of the attic, in which Rembrandt stood upright in his working tunic with his hands on his hips and appears defiant and invincible today to any onlooker who dares meet his eyes in the Kunsthistorisches Museum in Vienna.

Pensive torment he reserved for his paintings of others.

Joseph Heller
Picture This, 1988

Further Reading

Ainworth, Maryan W., and John Brealy, *Art and Autoradiography: Insights Into the Genesis of Paintings of Rembrandt, Van Dyke, and Vermeer*, The Metropolitan Museum of Art, New York, 1982

Alpers, Svetlana, *Rembrandt's Enterprise: The Studio and the Market*, Thames and Hudson, London, 1988

Benesch, Otto, *From an Art Historian's Workshop: Rembrandt, Dutch and Flemish Masters, Velásquez, Frederik Van*

Valckenborch*, Hacker Art Books, New York, 1979

———, *Rembrandt*, Rizzoli International, New York, 1990

Biorklund, George, and Osbert Barnard, *Rembrandt's Etchings*, Hacker Art Books, New York, 1988

Clark, Kenneth, *An Introduction to Rembrandt*, Harper and Row, New York, 1978

Fuchs, R. H., *Dutch Painting*, Thames and Hudson, London, 1978

Haak, Bob, *The Golden Age: Dutch Painters of the Seventeenth Century*, Thames and Hudson, London, 1984

———, *Rembrandt Drawings*, Thames and Hudson, London, 1984

Münz, Ludwig, and Bob Haak, *Rembrandt*, Harry N. Abrams, New York, 1984

Puppi, Lionello, *Rembrandt*, Thames and Hudson, London, 1969

Rembrandt Research Project Staff, *A Corpus of*

Rembrandt Paintings, Kluwer Academic, Norwell, Massachusetts, 1982

Rosenberg, Jakob, *Rembrandt: Life and Work*, Cornell University Press, Ithaca, 1980

Schneider, Cynthia P., *Rembrandt's Landscapes*, Yale University Press, New Haven, 1990

Van der Meulen, Marjon, and Walter L. Strauss, *The Rembrandt Documents*, Abaris Books, Pleasantville, New York, 1979

List of Illustrations

Index

Photograph Credits

All Rights Reserved 36–7, 124, 136. Amsterdam City Archives 110b. Armand Hammer Collection, Los Angeles 114, 115. Artephot/Brumaire, Paris 83b. Artephot/Cercle d'Art, Paris 51. Artephot/Faillet, Paris 26. Artephot/A. Held 29l, 30a, 30b, 31, 46–7, 48–9, 52l, 52r, 53, 54, 58, 59, 65, 68–9, 70, 92l, 94, 96, 99b, 100, 101, 103b, 104l, 105r, 106–7, 107, 111, 112–3a, 112–3b, 116–7, 124–5, 126, 126–7, 128, 141, 142, 162l, 167, front cover, spine, back cover. Artephot/Nimatallah, Paris 32, 33, 38, 99a, 123r. Artephot/Oronoz, Paris 56–7. Artephot/Reinhold, Paris 60. Artothek/J. Blauel, Peissenberg 113br. Bibliothèque Nationale, Paris 11, 13, 14a, 14b, 15, 17, 18b, 20b, 24b, 25a, 25b, 34bl, 35cr, 35b, 41, 55cr, 57, 61a, 67b, 71, 73l, 73r, 76, 80–1, 81ar, 81b, 82, 88a, 88–9, 90–1, 102l, 102c, 102r, 103al, 103ac, 103ar, 110a, 140, 150, 151, 154. Bildarchiv, Berlin 50. Boymans-van Beuningen Museum, Rotterdam 43, 117b. British Museum, London 85, 98, 159, 163r. Brod Gallery, London 28a. Ecole Nationale Supérieure des Beaux-Arts, Paris 36b. Edimédia, Paris 139. Gemeentemusea, Delft 46b. Giraudon, Paris 18a, 74–5, 119. Haags Gemeentemuseum, The Hague 21. Het Rembrandthuis, Amsterdam 62, 64. Historisch Museum, Amsterdam 46a. Lauros-Giraudon, Paris 27a. Magnum/Erich Lessing, Paris 36a, 62–3, 108–9, 109cr. Mauritshuis, The Hague 109c, 109br. The Metropolitan Museum of Art, New York 118, 165. Museum of Fine Arts, Boston 34–5. National Gallery, London 121. National Gallery of Art, Washington, D.C. 12. Norton Simon Foundation, Pasadena, California 84. Réunion des Musées Nationaux, Paris 19, 20a, 22–3, 24a, 28–9, 29r, 39, 40, 42l, 44–5, 54–5, 55a, 61b, 63ar, 66l, 72, 77b, 79, 83a, 86, 87, 89a, 90b, 92r, 93, 96–7, 97ar, 108l, 109ar, 138, 153, 157, 161, 166. Rijksmuseum, Amsterdam 1, 2–9, 16, 77a, 78, 148, 163l. Roger-Viollet, Paris 34br, 91r, 116, 127ar, 129, 130, 143, 144, 147, 149, 152, 156, 158, 162r. Scala, Antella 104–5, 122l, 122r, 123l. Gregory W. Schmitz, New York 27b. Staatliche Museen, Berlin 66–7, 95. Teylers Museum, Haarlem 80b

Text Credits

Grateful acknowledgment is made for permission to use material from the following works: Joseph Heller, *Picture This*, reprinted by permission of The Putnam Publishing Group, New York, copyright © 1988 by Joseph Heller (pp. 164–7); Rembrandt Research Project, Amsterdam, Kluwer Academic Publishers, Dordrecht, *A Corpus of Rembrandt Paintings*, Vol. 1, 1982 (pp. 160–3); Walter L. Strauss and Marjon van der Meulen (eds.), *The Rembrandt Documents*, pp. 129, 167, 173, 349–87, Abaris Books, Inc., Pleasantville, New York, 1979 (pp. 52–3, 61–2, 130–5); *The Complete Letters of Vincent van Gogh*, trans. by J. van Gogh-Bonger and C. de Dood, by permission of Thames and Hudson Ltd, London, and Little, Brown and Company, Boston, in conjunction with The New York Graphic Society, all rights reserved, 1958 (pp. 140–3)

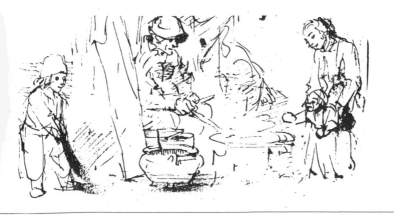

Pascal Bonafoux is an art historian and author whose works
include *Rembrandt, autoportrait,* winner of the 1985
Académie Française's Prix Charles-Blanc and
the Prix Elie Faure et Gutenberg. He is the author of
Van Gogh: The Passionate Eye
in the Discoveries series.

Translated from the French by Alexandra Campbell

Project Manager: Sharon AvRutick
Typographic Designer: Elissa Ichiyasu
Editorial Assistant: Jennifer Stockman
Design Assistant: Penelope Hardy

Library of Congress Catalog Card Number: 92–71190
ISBN 0–8109–2813–2

Copyright © 1990 Gallimard

English translation copyright © 1992 Harry N. Abrams, Inc., New York,
and Thames and Hudson Ltd., London

Published in 1992 by Harry N. Abrams, Incorporated, New York
A Times Mirror Company

Printed and bound in Italy by Editoriale Libraria, Trieste